Cooks of the British Virgin Islands

A CULINARY JOURNEY

JAN MORASH

First published in the United States
of America by:

Twin Lights Publishers, Inc.
10 Hale Street
Rockport, Massachusetts 01966
Telephone: (978) 546-7398
http://www.twinlightspub.com

ISBN 1-885435-49-5

10 9 8 7 6 5 4 3 2 1

Book design by:
SYP Design & Production, Inc.
www.sypdesign.com

Photography:
Susan Sheen, Steve Simonsen

Editorial:
Jan Morash

Printed in China

Introduction

Say BVI to anyone who will listen and you get back tales of sailing, sandy beaches, sun and snorkeling. When I first arrived thirty-five years ago food was the last thing on my rum-soaked brain. One simply did not think of this place as a foodie paradise, more of a desert actually.

Thirty-five years ago the typical visitor was a group of sailing buddies, usually men, bent on sailing hard and drinking even harder. There were a few fine restaurants, such as Little Dix, but to a group of unshaven sailors that was not a possibility. Back then you had to wear a jacket and we hardly wore shoes.

A fine restaurant would have been a difficult undertaking. Supplies and food were impossible to get and no one understood the concept of service. The story today is quite different. Many visitors come with their wives and families. They are as likely to stay in a four-star resort or rent an elegant villa, as they are to charter a boat. Even chartering has changed to include crewed vacations, where every detail is taken care of. Chefs and restaurateurs, sensing this shift soon followed. They opened their doors to an ever more sophisticated clientele. Some of the locals who worked in the early resorts and restaurants opened places of their own and often featured local menus. Locally famous cooks opened small places to serve the neighborhood, but as their reputation spread they grew. Food became part of the BVI scene. News of any new, good restaurant spread by word of mouth very quickly. The newest, best restaurant was constantly raising the bar.

Today the BVI is still one of the most beautiful places on the planet, but we can now say that the food holds its own in any company. In a tiny place like this we are blessed to have an enormous variety of fine restaurants. You can find everything from a good cheap burger to French Haute Cuisine.

This humble volume is neither a restaurant review nor a comprehensive BVI cookbook. It does represent the publisher's biases and opinions. As you pour through it you will, undoubtedly, scream in disgust that your favorite restaurant is not among the pages. I am sorry about that, but there are reasons. There are simply too many places to visit. There are only so many pages in the book. That said, the book does represent a good cross section of cooking in the BVI and should give you some great recipes.

The recipes in this book are presented as given to me by the chefs and cooks themselves. In the American and European tradition recipes are written and precise. In the West Indian tradition they are oral and contain such instructions as, "season until it is right." When I would ask what that meant the chef would answer, "you know— taste it and add till it's right." Recipes and methods are passed down within the family, which often means that the same dish is very different from place to place. As you try these dishes and you are in need of an opinion as to whether it is "right," call me and I'll come for dinner.

Bon Appetite,
Paul Sylva

Big Bamboo

ON LOBLOLLY BAY

It's the end of the road folks—literally—it comes this far and just stops. Why would you want to go any further? Most don't. This is their destination on Anegada and it has been since Big Bamboo was first established. It's the most famous of the Anegada restaurants and is recognized as the place for lobster in the whole of the BVI.

It took awhile to develop such an auspicious reputation in such an inaccessible location. Aubrey (island-born) and Dion (Trinidadian) Levons built their restaurant on his family's land in Loblolly Bay twenty-one years ago when tourism in Anegada was in its infancy; when each new guest who entered their premises was a blessing, and each returning customer, a triumph. Aubrey, an affable host, and Dion, the accomplished chef, employed their natural skills

with one and all. Soon word of Big Bamboo swelled and spread.

Though today, for many visitors, "a trip to Anegada" is synonymous with "lobster at Big Bamboo," dinners are by no means restricted to the delicacy. The varied menu carries numerous outstanding meat, poultry, and fish dishes (including Dion's crab cakes, which are almost as famous as the lobster). No matter what size party, there is something to entice and gratify each member.

Gone are the lean years when Big Bamboo saw maybe a dozen customers in a week. These days, full house is more the norm and experienced visitors know to call ahead with reservations.

Big bamboo is right on the beach at Loblolly Bay, a location known for its spectacular snorkeling.

BIG BAMBOO ON LOBLOLLY BAY

The Anegada-davida (drink)

Lyches
Coco Lopez (small amount)
Grenadine (small amount)
pineapple juice
Franjelico
Amaretto
white rum

Add ice and blend.

. . . .

Conch Stew
(4 servings)

Cut up onions, garlic and celery. Sauté in butter. Add lime. Add a little tomato paste (1 tsp.). Cut conchs in small bits with touch of Bohio Adobo Criollo (seasoning from Puerto Rico.....salt, garlic, oregano, tumeric). Simmer.

Chicken Wings

Clean chicken. In a bowl, mix small amount of vinegar, hot pepper sauce (Matouk's), salt, Bohio, and a little sugar. Chop onions and garlic and blend together. Add to mixture. Add black pepper and mix well. Cut up wings and soak in mixture for a day or two. Fry in oil.

Note: Use 5-oz. bottle of hot pepper sauce for 8 people. Here, the chef uses Matouk's hot pepper sauce, which is a salsa picante. You can serve the wings as they are, or with a sauce.

Biras Creek

One hundred and forty acres of tranquility and beauty, coupled with a world-class restaurant, is one of several ways to describe Biras Creek. Other adjectives that come to mind are relaxed, elegant, fun, and remote. The restaurant, which is situated on Virgin Gorda on a site accessible only by boat, retains an air of exclusive beauty. It is high on the property, affording a panoramic view of the ocean and the Sound. Few restaurants can rival Biras Creek when it comes to the view… and even fewer when you consider the food.

Chef Neil Hitchen and food and beverage manager Louise McCaffery run what many believe to be the best restaurant in the BVI. From the moment you sit down the service tells you that this place is special. The menu, a mix of American, European, and West Indian cuisines, changes almost daily. To call it creative is not to do it justice. The wine list, Louise's pride and joy, is extensive and well thought out, with many wines not available elsewhere.

Biras Creek is well worth sailing in or calling the restaurant for the ferry over. When you go, be sure to make a reservation if you're not planning on staying at the hotel. Also, allow enough time for a stroll about or a game of snooker. Snooker is located in a building that was built to hold the largest table in the West Indies.

Pan Seared Sea Bream with a Char-Grilled Tomato and Red Onion Salad and a Tomato and Basil Butter Sauce

4 fillets of sea bream
3 red onions
8 plum tomatoes
12 cherry tomatoes
chopped parsley
chopped basil
1 tsp. sherry vinegar
sugar to taste
1/2 cup cream
diced butter
olive oil
lemon juice

Blend four plum tomatoes with vinegar, sugar and basil. Strain through a sieve into a pan and reduce. Mix in cream and bring to heat. Whisk in the butter and chopped basil. Season. Set aside.

Cut the onion and remaining plum tomatoes in half. Toss in olive oil, garlic, parsley, salt and pepper, and place on a hot grill until soft.

Chop and mix together with olive oil and season. To roast the cherry tomatoes, warm olive oil in a pan. Add the cherry tomatoes, season with salt and pepper. Cook until soft but hold their shape.

Season fish, place in hot pan and sear until golden brown. Finish with lemon juice.To assemble dish, place red onion and tomato salad in the center of the plate. Place the fish fillets on top, three roasted tomatoes per person. Place sauce around the salad and garnish with a fresh basil leaf.

Brandade of Salt Fish with Salad Greens and a Chilled Gazpacho Sauce

1 lb. salt fish, soaked overnight in water
3 potatoes, cooked, mashed, and cooled
bay leaves
4 cloves garlic
1 bunch parsley, finely chopped
lemon juice to taste
fresh black pepper to taste
salad greens
gazpacho

Cover the salt fish in milk with two bay leaves, six black peppercorns and four cloves of garlic. Bring to a boil. Turn down heat and simmer gently until cooked.

Pick salt fish until all bones and skin are removed. Rinse the salt fish under cool water and squeeze until dry.

Add the mashed potatoes to the salt fish, parsley, lemon juice and pepper until firm.

To assemble: Using two spoons make quenelles with the salt fish mixture and place three on a plate. Dress the salad and place in the middle of the plate. Spoon the gazpacho dressing in between the quenelles. Garnish the brandade with dill sprigs.

Coconut Creme Caramel with Mango Puree and a Coconut Tuille

Ingredients for Caramel:
50 g. sugar
1/2 oz. water

Ingredients for Custard:
1/2 litre milk
100 g. sugar
3 eggs yolk
50 g. shredded coconut

Ingredients for Mango Puree:
1 ripe mango, peeled and chopped
2 oz. white wine
1 oz. sugar

Ingredients for Coconnt Tuille:
2 egg whites
4 oz. icing sugar
3 oz. flour
3 1/2 oz. melted butter
shredded coconut

To make the caramel: Place sugar and water in a pan. Cook until golden and place in desired mould.

To make the custard: Bring milk and half of the sugar to a boil. Remove from heat and let sit for five minutes. Whisk the other half of the sugar with the eggs. Add the slightly cooled milk to the egg mixture and whisk. Add coconut. Pour into the moulds and cook in low oven until set.

To make the puree: Place all ingredients in a blender. Blend until smooth.

To make the tuille: Whisk egg whites until firm. Slowly add icing sugar and whisk until glossy. Add melted butter and gently fold in flour and coconut. Spread mixture onto a greased sheet pan in desired shape. Bake until golden brown.

To assemble the dish: Spoon the mango puree into the center of the plate, place turned out creme caramel on top of the puree. Place coconut tuilles on top of creme caramel. Garnish with a sprig of mint and toasted coconut.

Bitter End
YACHT CLUB

When the hotel rooms at The Bitter End Yacht Club on Virgin Gorda are all taken and the moorings in the North Sound are at full occupancy, Executive Chef Trevor Nicely, along with his kitchen staff of up to twenty-five, caters to more diners in one evening than some local restaurants do in two or three weeks.

Trevor meets the challenge of such volume armed with the sound training and practice he gained in his native UK. His approach is practical, with buffet lunches and dinner carveries helping to supplement the regular menu. Trevor is also thorough in his attention to quality and detail. The menu features Caribbean cooking that is slightly moderated to suit the tastes and trends (such as low caloric content) of the largely American and European clientele.

Another brave commander in the battle of the numbers is Executive Pastry Chef Winston Butler. He began as a waiter from St. Vincent with dreams of becoming a pastry chef. After years of study at such prestigious schools as the Culinary Institute of America in New York, Johnson and Wales in Rhode Island, and the Polytechnic School of Baking in London, Butler realized his dreams. He now runs Bitter End's in-house bakery. There, each and every roll, slice of bread, piece of cake, and fancy pastry needed for the multitudes of diners is prepared daily.

So is quality sacrificed in the name of quantity? You could ask the hotel guests, but the fact that most of them have not only stayed here numerous times, but have also pre-booked for next year, pretty much answers the question.

The deck at the Bitter End may be the best place to watch a sunset in all of North Sound.

Below, pastry Chef Winston Butler struts his stuff.

Bitter End Pumpkin Soup

1 onion
5 celery stalks, sliced
2 carrots sliced
5 lbs. pumpkin
1 tsp. beef base
1 tsp. chicken base
2 cloves garlic
1 tsp. cinnamon
1 tsp. black pepper
1 gal. water

Peel the pumpkin and cut into pieces and steam. Place the remaining vegetables in the water and boil till very soft. Once ingredients are cooked, place in a blender and puree. After pureeing, pass through a sieve and adjust seasoning to taste.

Bitter End Lobster Salad

4 medium-sized whole lobsters
2 oz. green peppers
2 oz. onions
1 cup mayonnaise
salt, pepper
olive oil
1 tbsp. spicy pepper sauce of choice

Place whole lobsters into pan of water and bring to a boil and simmer for 4 to 5 minutes. Take lobsters out of water and place to cool. Chop onions and peppers and place in a bowl.

When lobsters are cooled, cut open and remove all the meat. Cut into bite-size pieces. Dice and combine all remaining ingredients.

Brandywine Bay
RESTAURANT

In the competitive realm of BVI dining, how do you get the reputation for being the best in the Territory? Davide Pugliese knows.

First, you have the sense to be born in Firenze, Italy where you grow up in a culture renowned for its reverence for good food. You study art, specifically photography, set up your own business, and eventually move to New York. While you enjoy success as a fashion photographer, you indulge your love of cooking by whipping up four-course meals for friends and colleagues after nerve-wracking photo shoots, and thus uncover an innate culinary talent that you decide is your true calling. You decide to open your own restaurant.

Next, you search for an exotic location; you find it in the BVI at Brandywine Bay on Tortola. Once the site of a fort built by the English to protect their holding, it commands an extensive view of the length of Sir Francis Drake Channel. Perfect.

Then, you open Brandywine Bay Restaurant. You decorate your premises with tasteful artist touches, stock an impressive supply of wine, build a friendly, knowledgeable staff, leave the front of the house to your lovely wife while you concentrate on creating the ever-changing, always amazing dishes (Italian and otherwise) that will become your trademark, and finally, you consider your customers to be diners in your own home.

And voila! You've got a hit! Simple, right Davide?

BRANDYWINE BAY RESTAURANT

Panna Cotta
(Serves 6)

1.5 dl milk (10 tablespoons)
3 sheets gelatin, soaked
1/2 lt heavy cream
50 g. powdered sugar
1 tsp. vanilla extract
1 shot dark rum
2 cups sugar
1 dl heavy cream (about 7 tablespoons)
1 tsp. lemon juice

Dissolve gelatin in warm milk.

Mix together the warm milk and dissolved gelatin with the heavy cream, powered sugar, vanilla extract and rum.

In a non-reactive pan mix the lemon juice with the sugar until the sugar has caramelized. Add the cream slowly to the sugar.

Coat 6 custard dishes with the caramelized sugar mixture. Pour the milk and gelatin mixture in each dish and place in refrigerator until set for a minimum of 3 hours.

Note: Can be served with a mango or passion fruit sauce.

Portabella Mushroom Napoleon
(serves 4)

4 portabella mushroom caps
1 cup polenta (uncooked)
4 slices fontina cheese
8 baby lettuce leaves (for garnish)

Cook polenta as per instructions. Spread out cooked polenta on a cookie pan so that it is about 1/2 inch thick. Allow it to cool (you can prepare this a day ahead).

Clean the portabella caps with a paper towel—don't use water. Brush mushrooms with olive oil so it absorbs some of the oil. Salt and pepper to taste. Grill under a very hot grill or broiler for 5 minutes on each side until done.

At the same time cut the polenta with a round cookie cutter just slightly smaller than the mushroom cap. Also grill the polenta, marking it with a cross as you do.

Place the mushrooms, skin side down, on a cookie sheet. Put the polenta on top of the mushrooms and then a slice of the fontina cheese. Melt the cheese under the grill.

Serve on the baby lettuce leaves.

Note: Remember mushrooms are like sponges—they will absorb any liquid they come into contact with, so when you brush them with the oil, just let the necessary amount be absorbed by them.

Porcini Crusted Tuna with a Balsamic Glaze
(Serves 4)

4 2" yellowfin tuna steaks
1/3 cup porcini mushroom powder
1/3 cup rice flour
1 tsb. butter
salt and pepper to taste
1 cup balsamic vinegar glaze (refer to recipe)

Have tuna steak cut from the core or use sushi grade tuna loin. Mix the porcini mushroom powder with the rice flour and salt and pepper.

Place a heavy cast iron skillet on a very high heat.

Dust the tuna steaks with the porcini/flour mix to coat them on the top and bottom sides. Place the butter in the skillet (it will flame) and sear the tuna for less than a 1/2 minute on each side until you have a crust on the tuna but it is still rare inside.

Slice the tuna on a bias and fan on the plate. Drizzle with Balsamic Vinegar Glaze and serve with rice.

Note: If you can't find the porcini mushroom powder, use dry porcini and grind them to a fine powder in a spice grinder.

. . . .

Balsamic Vinegar Glaze

3 cups balsamic vinegar
1/2 cup honey

Combine the vinegar and honey in a saucepan and bring to a boil. Reduce until it is equivalent to 1 cup. Refrigerate (this glaze will keep for a long time).

Before serving bring the glaze to room temperature. It should be very thick and be able to coat a spoon and drip like honey.

C&F

RESTAURANT

The BVI is still a relatively new discovery as a holiday getaway when compared to such destinations as Bermuda, Antigua or Saint Lucia. Once discovered, however, visitors tend to return, drawn to the unspoiled beauty of these islands.

First-timers to Tortolla don't always find C&F, but return visitors inevitably track it down and make it a permanent item on their annual holiday itineraries. The main attraction, besides Clarence (the C) and his wife Florina (the F), is their famous BBQ. Ribs, fish, and, of course, chicken, sizzle over the flames of the huge modern pit. The pit has replaced the oil drums of the past, but still burns charcoal made from the wood of local farmers.

"I was the first one to use the oil drum to barbecue in the BVI," Clarence claims. This would have been in 1986 when he, a St. Lucian, met Florina in St. Croix and followed her here. Back then, C&F was open once a week for take-out BBQ, but demand soon dictated a much more ambitious schedule. Today, dinner is available seven nights a week and ten months of the year. "My social life is in September and October," Clarence explains. But their efforts are rewarded by an ever-growing list of both foreign and local customers. They are also proud to be four-time recipients of the Best Food in the BVI Award. Well done.

Chef Clarence IS the grill master, as anyone whoever had his ribs will tell you.

Callaloo
ON THE BEACH

Leasa Binns is the driving force at Callaloo on the Beach. Although she is a chef, her enthusiasm does not restrict itself to the kitchen. "You might see me working the front desk or waiting the tables. I'm all over." A young woman of many talents, it is her talent for cooking that won her the Service Professional of the Year award for the Caribbean in the year 2000. Her coconut crêpes with caramelised banana in coffee liqueur was the key to impressing the judges, but her lively personality and obvious passion for her craft couldn't have hurt.

Leasa got her initial training and experience in Jamaica, her homeland. However she credits Andre Nederhouser with teaching her international cooking. "I would fantasize that some day I would be able to cook like that man. I watched and watched him and I practised and practised." It was Andre, Prospect Reef's G M at the time, who found Leasa in Jamaica and brought her to the BVI. He taught her to "cook on the spot" or apply one's skills to any given set of food items and produce the best possible dish. This is a skill that Leasa has taken to heart. She devours recipes from books and has many in her head from home, but the recipes she uses are her own. The results are the gourmet meals served at Callaloo on the Beach.

Visitors can come to Prospect Reef on Tortola and be ferried over to the restaurant on Peter Island. Once on the island you can stay for a meal or just a day on the beach.

Diners can enjoy the view of Great Harbor at Callaloo, while Leasa's smile brings the sunshine to the open kitchen.

Coconut Crêpes with Carmelized Banana in Coffee Liqueur

Coconut Crêpes:
5 eggs
6 oz. flour
2 oz. sugar
2 1/2 cups milk
1 oz. coconut flakes

. . . .

Filling:
Carmelized Banana in Coffee Liquer
6 ripe bananas
4 oz. brown sugar
1 tsp. nutmeg and cinnamon mix
2 tbs. lemon juice
butter
3 oz. coffee liqueur

Sauté until tender.

Leasa's Mango Chutney

4 mangos
2 oz. white raisins
1 yellow onion
fresh thyme
3 oz. passion fruit juice concentrated
1 1/2 oz. white vinegar
2 oz. white wine
5 oz. brown sugar
special seasoning salt mix

Chez Bamboo

If you took a little European Bistro, jazzed it up with some funky artwork and a New York style martini bar, and set it down on a little patch of tropical jungle on the side of the road in Virgin Gorda, you would have Chez Bamboo.

This was Rose Giacinto's vision. Owner of the popular Bath and Turtle Pub on Virgin Gorda, Rose always wanted something a little simpler, but still with a bit of style. She also knew where she wanted it to be. "Whenever I passed the building [which housed a French restaurant at the time], I wanted to get a hold of it. I knew I could do something with it."

Rose's opportunity came in 1995. That year, she bought the building and began its transformation. She started by adding splashes of color inside and out, and then built and furnished an outside terrace with a mini-jungle around it. Finally, she draped fairy lights here and there. In the end she created a magical atmosphere that everyone wanted to check out.

The creative ideas didn't stop at the decorations. The menu is a unique array of French and Caribbean dishes executed by Chef Joycee McLeary. It features such gems as Nassau Grouper in Papillote, Lobster Curry, and Spicy BBQ shrimp. The martini bar serves twelve (and counting) different kinds of martinis including espresso, lemon drop, and the bikini martini.

Though her background is in the fashion industries of Texas and New York, Rose was no stranger to the BVI or to the restaurant business when she created Chez Bamboo. She and her late husband, Mike, had been coming here for years and were involved in the management of several local establishments before buying the B&T.

With her blend of experience and original ideas, Rose has added a touch of chic to the restaurant scene in the BVI.

Nassau Grouper in Papillote

4 grouper fillets
5 celery stalks, chopped
4 shallots, chopped
8 shrimp
1 cup lobster meat
1/2 cup crab meat
sea salt and pepper to taste
1/2 cup white wine
1/2 cup heavy cream
chopped parsley

Sauté celery and shallots in 2 tbsp. butter. Add seafood and white wine until reduced. Add cream and seasoning. Cut rounds of parchment paper. Add a piece of grouper on each paper. Divide sauce evenly over each piece of fish. Sprinkle with parsley. Close up each parcel securing contents, twisting the paper on the sides. Bake on baking sheet for 15-20 minutes. Serve in paper parcels.

. . . .

Leonard's Espresso Martini

1/2 oz. Absolute vanilla vodka
1/4 oz. Tia Maria
4 oz. espresso

Put into a shaker and shake vigorously. Pour into martini glasses.

Warm Chocolate Molten Cake

6 oz. bittersweet chocolate
12 tbsp. unsalted butter (room temperature)
2/3 cup sugar
1 2/3 cup finely ground pecans
4 eggs, separated

Icing:
3 1/2 oz. bittersweet chocolate
3 tbsp. butter

Preheat oven to 350 degrees. Line a 10-inch spring form pan with parchment paper. Chop chocolate and melt in a double boiler. Cream butter together with sugar. Add ground pecans, egg yolks and melted chocolate and beat well. Whisk together egg whites until stiff and fold into mixture. Pour into baking pan. Bake 35 minutes. Let cool and cover in icing.

The quiet interior of Chez Bamboo and the lovely martini bar are reminiscent of New York, but dining in the garden brings you back to the West Indies.

Cow Wreck Beach

RESTAURANT & GRILL

Secluded in the most remote location on Anegada, Cow Wreck Beach Restaurant & Grill is surrounded by sand dunes, palm trees, cows, wild donkeys, and of course, the sea. It is no surprise that the owner, Belle Creque, is a native of the island. An outsider would probably never have found it or had faith that future customers would. However, Belle's faith was well founded. "I started with two tables that seated eight people and a kitchen the size of a closet." Now, eight years later, Belle has a large kitchen and can serve much bigger groups (up to one hundred and fifty for functions).

Living in the U.S., Belle was dissatisfied with her job as a bookkeeper and decided to learn the restaurant trade. She loved it. After ten years of training and experience, she returned to Anegada and built her own business. It includes a bar, restaurant, guest accommodation (two little villas on the beach), and equipment rental (bicycles and kayaks).

Belle is kept busiest in the kitchen. Her customers come for the West Indian cooking, specifically the local Anegada fish dishes. She is also quickly becoming revered for her homemade fruit pies. So where does Belle get the customers in such an isolated locale? She imports them. Yachtsmen, sailing into Anegada, simply contact her by VHF and a boat is sent to ferry them in. They come for the food, they come for the hospitality, and they come for a welcome getaway.

COW WRECK BEACH

Stewed Coconut Tart

Crust:
8 eggs
2 lbs. margarine
1 lb. Crisco
1 12-oz. can Carnation milk
1 litre long-life milk
3 tbsp. baking powder
dash vanilla
dash almond
flour to desired texture

. . . .

Filling:
grated coconuts (2)
2 lbs. sugar
dash vanilla
dash almond
cinnamon stick
1 cup water
Stew to desired texture. Cook the shell at 350° for 15-20
minutes. Add the warm filling and chill.

Local Anegada Conch

Stewed Conch:
Cut conch to desired thickness and pressure cook to
desired softness.

Cut up:
1 onion
1/2 green pepper
stick celery
2 tbsp. margarine
2 tbsp. tomato sauce

Put in sauce pan. Season to taste. Bring to a boil.
Serve with white rice, rice and beans and plantain.

Coco Plums

AT BOMBA SHACK

The Molyneaux brothers, Curt, Mitch, and Daz, left Tortola as toddlers. Now, they have blown back into town some thirty-odd years later vowing to corner the BVI restaurant market. Everyone is curious. Many are doubtful. The brothers assure their detractors that they are indeed chefs, and they rattle off a resume of a cumulative sixty-four years of experience cooking in every well-known highbrow establishment in America. Of course no one believes them, but the brothers don't mind.

The brothers' restaurant, Coco Plums at Bomba Shack, is located in Apple Bay. To the amazement of everyone, including their famous uncle from across the street at Bomba Shack, the restaurant has had a very successful first season. "I think he was shocked," laughs Mitch. Now the naysayers don't know what to think. However, a visit to Coco Plums proves that the brothers definitely know their stuff. The food is impressive, imaginative, very tasty, and what's more, it's inexpensive.

The evident talent and exuberant confidence of the Molyneaux brothers makes even sceptics admit that the boys are well on their way to making good on their vow. In fact, they have a second restaurant location on the way!

The Bomba Shack is made from materials washed up on the beach. It is one of the all time greatest party scenes in the BVI. A full moon party here is something no one ever forgets.

Courtyard Coffee Shoppe

In the midst of the relative hustle and bustle of Road Town, tucked among the businesses and tourist traps of Main Street, is a refuge called The Courtyard Coffee Shoppe. A single glance reveals a bright little Caribbean building that evokes the old world charm of Road Town from centuries past. Inside the building one finds an array of coffees that rivals the modern metropolitan cafés of Boston and New York.

There are teas too, as you would expect, but most go for a cappuccino or latte. Then there are the pastries: confectionaries and West Indian meat patties. Finally, you have a choice of books and magazines to browse through as you sip and nibble in the sheltered courtyard.

Proprietor Philip Fenty came to Tortola from Grenada eighteen years ago as an employee of Barclay's Bank. On semi-retirement he opened the coffee shop, knowing full well of the need for a pick-me-up and safe haven in the business section of town.

When he found the little house on Main Street it was derelict. Built by A.O. Shirley's father in the early 1920's, its original timber was still intact. Philip was careful to preserve its mortise and tenet construction in the restoration.

There is talk of a Renaissance Main Street in Road Town. Hopefully, The Courtyard Coffee Shoppe is a forerunner of more to come.

Philip Fenty has created an oasis in the middle of busy Road Town. It is a quiet and restful place to spend some time and the drinks are wonderful. Having a chat with Philip is an exercise in tranquility. It is hard to believe that the bustle of the capital is right outside the door.

De Loose Mongoose

RESTAURANT AND BAR

De Loose Mongoose, a beach bar/restaurant, is mere yards from the water's edge in Trellis Bay. It looks like it's always been there under the protective cover of the leaning coconut palms. Though faithful customers have seen some changes over the years as management and staff have come and gone, De Loose Mongoose remains a favourite hangout for locals and returning tourists alike.

One of the driving forces behind its great success these days is, indisputably, Rose the night chef. Although she has only been there for eight years, she already seems to be a permanent fixture in the restaurant. Rose runs a tight kitchen that serves as many as one hundred plus dinners in an evening. The food and drink are exemplary all day long under the management of Simon, Caroline, and Mary, the day

chef. However, it is Rose who brings the customers back at night.

Born in St. Lucia, Rose Volney-Simon grew up near the Pitons, the island's once-active twin volcanoes. She first arrived in the BVI twenty-three years ago with her husband. Rose got her training in France and her local experience at The Conch Shell restaurant in Tortola. Like many West Indian women, Rose is that wonderful mix of no-nonsense briskness tempered by a motherly warmth that makes her reputably the best hugger in the BVI. However, there is nothing motherly about her famous rendition of The Big Bamboo when she comes out of the kitchen to entertain the crowds. She is as bubbly and sometimes as volatile as the Pitons in her native St. Lucia.

Rose holds sway in the kitchen except when there is music and the orders slow down. Then you will find this smiling lady on the dance floor. She dances as well as she cooks, which is to say very well. When the joint is jumping people dance inside, outside, on the dock and on the beach. This is one of the all time great beach bars in the BVI.

No See Um Cocktail

151 Rum
fruit punch
Coco Lopez (cream of coconut)
pineapple juice
fresh banana

Mix ingredients and blend with ice.

. . . .

West Indian Conch Stew
(Serves four)

3 lbs. cleaned conch
1 medium onion
1 red pepper
1 green pepper
2 cups tomato juice
hot pepper sauce
garlic

Tenderize conch in pressure cooker with 3 cloves of garlic for approximately half an hour. Chop onion, red and green pepper and lightly sauté in a saucepan. Add a good spoon of hot pepper sauce and 2 cups tomato juice. Add conch and let simmer for 10-15 minutes.

Season to taste. Serve with rice and peas.

Trash Omelet
(Serves one hungry person)

3 slices cooked bacon
2 cooked sausages
diced onion
diced red pepper
diced green pepper
1 slice each cooked turkey and ham
cheese
3 eggs
salt and pepper to taste

Fry onion and pepper in some butter. Chop and add other ingredients except cheese. Whisk eggs and add to skillet. Cook for 3 to 5 minutes until set, add cheese and fold in half. Cook for 3 to 5 minutes while cheese melts.

Serve with toast, butter and jelly with a fruit garnish.

Dixie's

Cammel Williams came to Virgin Gorda from Antigua nearly forty years ago. He worked on supply ships out of St. Thomas before landing a job at Little Dix as a dishwasher. There, he worked his way up through the ranks, was sent to numerous resorts and culinary schools in the U.S. (Woodstock Inn in Vermont and the Culinary Institute of America in New York), and eventually gained the position of Assistant Chef.

In 1985 Cammel decided to strike out on his own by opening Dixie's, Virgin Gorda's first takeout place. He specialized in chicken. "I had done a lot of traveling in the States and had seen that no matter where you go people eat chicken." He had also witnessed the success of fast food style takeaways and decided to try it here at home. It worked.

Dixie's has evolved to include inside and outside seating, non-chicken menu items, and daily specials. The food is superior to your average takeout (particularly the signature chicken), the service is friendly and fast, and the prices can't be beat.

People have been heard to say, "Thank God for Dixie's!"—workers with short lunch breaks, single people who can't be bothered to cook for one, working mothers who don't have the time to cook for many, and tourists who don't always want to eat in gourmet restaurants.

I say we should thank Cammel for Dixie's. It was his idea—although it could very well have been a divinely inspired one.

Creole Conch

10 lbs. conch, clean and cut in strips, cook until tender
dice:
  garlic
  onions
  celery
  green pepper
  red pepper
3 tbsp. olive oil or margarine
2 tins (3 oz.) mushrooms
2 tins stewed or fresh tomatoes
1 tin ketchup
2 tbsp. hot sauce
2 tins tomato sauce
1 cup sugar

Make creole sauce and add some of the juice from the conch to the sauce. Season with salt and pepper. Serve with white rice.

Caribbean Pumpkin Soup with Diced Chicken

diced chicken	carrots
peel and dice:	thyme leaf
pumpkin	celery
white potatoes	onions
sweet potatoes	garlic

Cook diced chicken and pumpkin, onions, garlic, carrots, celery, hot pepper and thyme, white potatoes, sweet potatoes and dumpling.

. . . .

Hot Pepper Sauce

onions	vinegar
garlic	3 tablespoons corn oil
hot peppers	mustard
salt	

Grind onions, garlic, hot peppers and vinegar, salt, mustard. Heat corn oil and add to it to bring out flavour.

Donovan's Reef

Jim and Bob McManus, native Pennsylvanians, first visited the BVI in 1994. They were so taken by the weather and the people of the BVI that they moved here to set up shop.

Shop is Donovan's Reef, a restaurant on Scrub Island that was built and outfitted by the brothers with the help of a friend from Johannesburg. The striking architecture, the gorgeous teak furniture made from the sleeper rails of the old South African-Zimbabwe railway lines, and the African artwork, give the restaurant a very unique, aesthetic character. The ambiance is further enhanced by the graciousness of the hosts and their staff.

From day one the restaurant has received attention and rave reviews, with many compliments going to the chef. That would be Chef Dwight. Born in St. Kitts, trained in the Caribbean and America, and experienced in Caribbean hotels, Dwight naturally adds a West Indian flare to the International style cuisine he prepares at Donovan's Reef. For example, his fish served with a sea grape sauce. "I add a little sunshine for the tourists to take home with them," he jokes.

Dwight is a happy man, living in Tortola with his wife, a nursing midwife, and their three children. "I love my wife and I love cooking," he says with a grin. Maybe his obvious happiness is the secret ingredient that puts his cooking at the top end of the "BVI's Best."

Donovan's Reef is one of the most beautiful places to enjoy a meal anywhere. The fact that it is on a private island makes it even more special. If you call them on the VHF radio or landline they will send a boat for you. The setting and the food make this worth the extra journey.

Donovan's Reef Pepper Pot Soup With Chicken

1 cup chopped okra
1 carrot peeled and diced
1 stalk celery diced
1 onion diced
thyme
1 cup chopped spinach
4 cups chicken broth
1/4 cup flour
1/4 cup butter
1 boneless chicken breast diced
1 bay leaf
pepper sauce
juice of 1 lime
1 cup heavy cream
salt and pepper

In a 2-quart pot, cook the butter and flour for 2 minutes. Add chicken broth. Salt and pepper to taste.

In another pot, sauté the onion, celery, carrot, thyme, okra, and chicken for a few minutes. Add the thickened broth to the vegetables and bring to a boil. Add the bay leaf, pepper sauce and lime juice. Add the spinach and cream just before serving.

. . . .

Donovan's Reef Grape Sauce

1 cup grapes - local if possible
2 shallots chopped
2 sprigs thyme
1 cup red wine
1/4 cup butter
1/2 cup guava puree
1 tsp. heavy cream

In a sauce pan combine grapes, shallots, thyme, and wine and reduce to 1/2 over medium heat. Add the cream and butter and whip, bit by bit until it thickens. Strain and add guava puree and keep warm until serving.

Perfect over fish or chicken.

Donovan's Reef Roulade of Chicken Breast

2 medium chicken breasts — whole (1 1/2 lbs. total)
1 cup crab meat
1/2 cup heavy cream
1 small onion diced
1 celery stick diced
2 cloves of garlic diced
3/4 cup parmesan cheese
1 cup flour
2 cups bread crumbs
2 large eggs
1/4 cup melted butter
salt and pepper to taste

Rinse chicken and pat dry. Place chicken between two pieces of plastic wrap and pound lightly until 1/8 inch thick. Sprinkle with salt and pepper.

In a sauce pan add the butter, onion, celery and garlic and sauté for two minutes. Add 1/2 the flour and stir to make a roux. Add the flour slowly and stir to make a cream sauce. Add the cheese and crabmeat and set aside to cool.

Stuff the chicken and roll. Dip in the remaining flour and lightly beaten eggs and bread crumbs. Cook at 375 degrees.

Eclipse

Grazing is a new trend in the BVI. Well, it's new to the local restaurant industry; the goats have been doing it here for centuries. Grazing refers to nibbling and sampling a variety of foods, rather than tucking into one particular dish. It is a very social approach to dining, as members of a party can order and indulge as a group.

Eclipse restaurant, at Penn's Landing in East End Tortola, has recently introduced the genre to the Territory and it is definitely catching on. The grazing menu includes a wide selection of ethnic cuisine: Caribbean, European, Indian, and Asian. The dishes come in generous portions suitable for sharing, while the entrée menu maintains more traditional dishes such as steak and swordfish. All are beautifully prepared and presented and can be matched with just the right wine from the comprehensive wine list.

BJ Turnbull, a Canadian, and Andy Dobbie, an American, met here in the BVI and formed their partnership. Together they bought Eclipse, which they co-own and manage. The present recipes are BJ's, whose early education in the trade began in his aunt and uncle's restaurant in Ontario, where he was truly inspired: "I soon learned that the chefs get all the cute waitresses. That was my original motivation."

Andy and BJ really know how to do a restaurant. With boats at the docks only a few feet away, you could picture yourself on the afterdeck of a yacht with your own chef and wait staff.

Sesame Seared Tuna Carpaccio

4 oz. piece of yellowfin tuna
1/2 cup sesame oil, plus 1 tbsp.
tsp. black sesame seeds

In a shallow bowl, toss the tuna, tbsp. sesame oil, and
the black sesame seeds until the tuna is coated evenly.
Wrap the tuna tightly with cling film and freeze.
Remove tuna from freezer and let stand for 20 minutes.

While the tuna stands, heat the 1/2 cup of sesame oil in
a shallow pan over high heat. When the oil has just
begun to smoke, turn off the heat, add the tuna and
quickly sear on all sides.

Slice the tuna as thinly as possible and garnish with
crispy wontons, pickled ginger, wasabi and marinated
cucumber.

Pistachio Encrusted Salmon with Truffle Oil and Balsamic/Pineapple Reduction

6-8oz. salmon fillets
1/2 cup shelled pistachios, finely crushed
1/4 cup balsamic vinegar
1/4 cup red wine
1/4 cup pineapple juice
tbsp. oilve oil
truffle oil
salt and pepper

For the salmon:
Season the salmon with salt and pepper. Coat on all sides
with the pistachios. In a heavy skillet, heat the olive oil
over medium heat and sear the salmon on all sides until
the pistachios are slightly browned. Place the fish in a
350 F oven for 5 minutes. Remove from oven and let
stand for 5 minutes more. Drizzle with truffle oil and the
balsamic/pineapple reduction

For the reduction:
Pour the balsamic vinegar, red wine and pineapple juice
in a sauce pan and simmer over low heat until reduced
by 3/4. Allow to cool before use.

Coconut Shrimp with Fried Plantains and Coconut Rum Sauce

4 16/20 prawns
1/2 cup shredded coconut
1/4 cup bread crumbs
1 egg
1/4 cup heavy cream
1/4 flour
2 cups peanut or vegetable oil
1 ripe plantain
1 green plantain
1 small onion
1 cup coconut rum
1 cup heavy cream
pepper to taste

For the shrimp:
Whisk together the egg and cream. Mix the shredded coconut and bread crumbs. Dredge the shrimp in the flour, then dunk into the egg/cream mixture, then coat with the coconut/bread crumb mixture.

Slice 5 peices of the ripe plantain crosswise with an angle about a 1/4 inch thick. With a vegetable peeler, pare 3 slices of the green plantain lengthwise.

Heat the oil in a heavy skillet to about 350 F. Cook the shrimp in the oil until golden brown, the ripe plantain until softened, and the green plantain until crisp. Arrange on a plate with the ripe plantains and garnish with the crisp green plantains.

Serve with the coconut rum sauce.

For the sauce:
Dice the onion and cook with the pepper in a saucepan with a little olive oil, do NOT brown. Away from the heat add the coconut rum and heavy cream. Return to heat and simmer until reduced by half. Allow to cool.

Grilled Duck Breast with Sautéed Spinach and Red Currant/Port Wine Sauce

6 oz. duck breast, trimmed and scored
1 small onion, diced
clove of garlic, minced
handful of fresh spinach
salt and pepper to taste
olive oil
1 tbsp. red currant jelly
1 tsp. crushed ginger root
pinch of cayenne pepper
1/2 cup port wine
1/4 cup veal jus
zest of lemon

For the duck:
Grill the duck breast 4 minutes on each side. Sauté the spinach with a little of the onion, garlic, and salt and pepper. Pile the spinach in the center of a plate. Slice the duck breast thinly and arrange around the spinach. Drizzle with the red currant/port wine sauce.

For the sauce:
Sauté the rest of the onion in a sauce pan with olive oil, jelly, ginger, and cayenne pepper. Melt over medium heat. Add port wine, veal jus and the zest of lemon and simmer until reduced by half. Allow to cool.

Escapade X

Escapade X is a yacht found most often in Trellis Bay. Although not a public restaurant, it boasts one of the most creative cooks in the BVI. Heather Hamilton and her husband John have prepared many fantastic meals over the years. The recipes included here are two favorites, extracted by force from Heather's collection. One cannot imagine the joy of sitting in the cockpit of Escapade X and sipping some good red wine while the aroma of these pasta dishes curls up from the galley and Heather pops up to refill your glass.

There is always good conversation and much laughter when you visit these Canadians. If you run into Heather at happy hour at De Loose Mongoose or at the Last Resort maybe you could get her to tell you that great chicken thing she does.

Penne a la Vodka

1/2 cup vodka
1 tbsp. red pepper flakes (or to taste)
1/2 butter
1 cup cream (heavy, light, or sour)
1 can (15 oz) diced tomatoes with juice
1 lb. penne pasta (cooked)
fresh basil leaves (optional)
1/2 cup fresh parmesan cheese

Marinate pepper flakes in vodka 2 to 3 hours. Strain to remove flakes and pour into a medium non-stick skillet. Heat over high heat, light the vodka and allow to burn till the flame goes out. Reduce heat to medium and add butter and cream. Stir and heat to a light rolling simmer. Add tomatoes, stir and heat through.* Season with salt and pepper. Toss with cooked pasta and serve with fresh basil and parmesan cheese.

*If it curdles, add flour and stir.

Rao' s Pasta

1/4 cup oil
1 lb. Italian sausage (hot or mild)
1 lb. savoy (or regular) cabbage
1 onion, chopped
4 cloves garlic, minced
1 lb. penne pasta, cooked
3 cups marinara sauce
salt and pepper to taste

Cook sausage, remove from pan and drain well. Sauté onion and garlic until clear. Add cabbage and sausage and cook all approximately 5 minutes. Add sauce and cook 10 minutes.

Add 1/2 to 1 cup sauce to cooked pasta and toss. Place pasta in bowl and distribute balance of sauce. Serve with freshly grated Romano cheese.

Fat Virgin Café

In 1493 Christopher Columbus named the third largest of the British Virgin Islands: Virgin Gorda, meaning Fat Virgin. Five hundred years later, Esther Wheatley chose the same name for her café. She believes in tradition.

Many of the BVI restaurants promote the Caribbean with their choice of menu, décor, and entertainment. Yet they proudly proclaim their fast, efficient service. Not Esther. "We move slowly in the Caribbean," she states unapologetically. "We want our guests to unplug at the airport - to relax, slow down, and experience the Caribbean that they came for in the first place."

Everything about the Fat Virgin Café invites their guests to do just that. The menu doesn't just feature Caribbean food, although it does so admirably with such offerings as guava-glazed ribs and fresh pan-fried snapper. It gently educates the novice Caribbean diner by slipping in traditional side dishes, such as roti on Monday night, and condiments like home-made pepper jelly. The selections are available all day, every day. You do not have to watch the clock to meet lunchtimes or dinnertimes. That is a North American or European concept, not a Caribbean one.

The focus of the Fat Virgin Café is on smaller, better, and true local. The setting in Biras Creek, at the far end of the North Sound, is peaceful and removed from any hustle-bustle. The staff is allowed to be who they are and, sure enough, guests respond and return. Customers forget the frenetic pace they left behind and open their eyes and hearts, for a little while, to Caribbean culture.

Don't let the small building or the humble location on the Biras Creek service dock, fool you. This place is first rate. Owner Esther Wheatly and chefs Pearl and Monica make this place a favorite of sailors. Landlubbers should take the 6:30 Biras ferry from Gun Creek and get off at the Fat Virgin.

Banana Cake

(Enough for one 10-inch spring pan)

Cream:
7 oz. of butter
3/4 cup light brown sugar
3/4 cup white sugar

When mixture is light and creamy add:
3 eggs (1 at a time)
5 small-medium bananas
1 tbsp. vanilla extract

In separate bowl:
3 cups of flour
1 1/2 tsp. of baking soda
3/4 tsp. of salt

the zest of 3 oranges (finely chopped)
1 cup of coursely chopped cashews

Combine with creamed mixture and bake until done in center.

Topping For Banana Cake:
1/4 pound of butter
1/2 cup brown sugar
vanilla
boil and add 1/2 cup of milk
rum
1 pureed banana

Let boil then coat the banana cashew cake.

. . . .

Golden Apple Chutney (Pineapple or Mangoes)

12 cups of peeled chopped golden apples

Boil:
5 1/2 cups of sugar
2 cups white vinegar
8 cups water

Let boil rapidly and add:
1 clove minced garlic
1 large onion, minced
5 tsp. Scotch Bonnel pepper
4 heaping tbsp. yellow mustard
1 cup vanilla extract*
1 2 or 3-inch flat cinnamon stick
1 heaping tsp. ground cinnamon
1 whole nutmeg, grated
1/2 piece of orange rind
1 heaping tsp. ground ginger

*1 cup vanilla is correct

Let all mixture continue to boil until it is a thick simple syrup and can coat a wooden spoon. Add 12 cups of golden apple and let it continue to cook at a rapid boil for another 20 minutes.

Note: Liquid mixture should be reduce by 1/2 before adding fruit .

Oriental Dressing

In a food processor or blender mince:
3-4 large shallots
5 cloves garlic
juice of 1 lemon
1/4 cup of rice vinegar or white vinegar
1/2 cup plus 3 soup spoons of Harveys Bristol Cream
1/2 cup water

Puree all together then add:
1 cup sesame tahini
1 cup teriyaki sauce
1/2 cup soy sauce (tamari)
1/2 cup light brown sugar
1/2 cup vegetable oil or sunflower oil

Blend all ingredients until smooth. Add:
5 tbsp. finely chopped parsley
2 heaping soup spoons finely grated ginger (no hairs)

Chill until ready to use.

Foxy's Tamarind
BAR & GRILL

Foxy Callwood is a local legend whose story has been told and written many times in various venues. He has entertained his guests at Foxy's Tamarind Bar and Grill with his songs and wit for nearly forty years. In the early days, he and his wife Tessa provided the food as well. These days Beverly Martin runs the food end of the operation. She met the Callwoods in 1971 while on holiday in the BVI from Washington, DC. Six months later she moved down and joined the team.

There have been changes in the restaurant over the years, going so far as closing down for a few years and then reopening to serve only lunches. Today, it has evolved into a full-blown restaurant, doing 150–180 covers per night in season. Don't worry; they still do their BBQ on Friday and Saturday nights. "We attempted to change that. We were getting a bit tired of it," Beverly admits, "but we met with a fair amount of resistance." Obviously the customers are not tired of the BBQ.

Foxy also produces his own beer, with four brands to date. The motivation behind the brewery's manufacturing of draught beer was to cut down on bottle usage and, consequently, trash on the islands.

Justine Callwood is Foxy's daughter. She has just opened a new restaurant at the far east end of Jost van Dyke, called Foxy's Taboo. Taboo was the old black lab of a song made famous in one of Foxy's ballads. The menu is mainly Mediterranean and is executed by a fine chef out of St. Thomas, J.F. Hawkins. "We want to address a gap that exists in the market," she explains. "We don't want to duplicate Foxy's [Tamarind]. We wouldn't want to cannibalise our own business. Hopefully, our customers will come to both."

Foxy Callwood has his own brand of rum, known as firewater. Ask him about it and his homemade beer when you visit the most famous bar in the Caribbean. Go in the afternoon and you will catch him, guitar in hand, singing and telling stories.

Grilled Swordfish with a Mango Salsa

Salsa:
Chop up the following:

2 ripe mangos
1/2 small red onion
1/2 red pepper
1 tsp. jalapeño pepper
1 tbsp. chopped cilantro
1/4 cup passion fruit juice
salt and pepper to taste

Marinade for Swordfish:
1 tbsp. fresh thyme
1 tbsp. paprika
3 cloves garlic
1 tbsp. fresh lime juice
2 dashes tabasco sauce
2 dashes Worcestershire sauce
1/2 cup olive oil

Marinate swordfish (8 oz. portion per person) for 1/2 hour. Sear on a flat grill on both sides for about 3 minutes per side. Place on plate and spoon about 1/4 cup salsa over the top of each portion of swordfish.

. . . .

Mussels in a Mustard Cream Sauce

4 cups Prince Edward Island mussels
1 cup white wine

Sauce:
2 tsp. chopped shallots
1 tsp. chopped garlic
1/2 cup white wine
1/2 cup whole grain mustard
2 cups heavy cream
2 tsp. cornstarch
1/4 cup water
salt and pepper to taste

In a saucepan combine shallots, garlic and white wine. Reduce to half over a medium flame. Add heavy cream and mustard. Bring to a boil. Add salt and pepper to taste.

Combine cornstarch and water to use as a thickener. Add to sauce to thicken. Set aside.

Steam mussels in shells in a wok or shallow frying pan in the white wine until shell opens.

Pour sauce over the mussels and serve.

. . . .

Banana Cheesecake

Crust:
1 box Ritz Crackers
6 oz. melted unsalted butter
1/2 cup sugar

Filling:
2 lbs. cream cheese
1-1/2 bananas
1 cup sugar
1/2 cup banana liqueur
2 tsp. vanilla extract
8 eggs

Topping:
1-1/2 cup sour cream
1/4 cup banana liqueur
1 tsp. vanilla extract
3 tbsp. sugar

Combine ingredients for crust in food processor and press into 10-inch spring form cake pan.

Mix filling ingredients in food processor until smooth and creamy. Pour into prepared cake pan. Bake in pre-heated oven at 350 degrees for 1 hour.

Whip topping and pour over baked cheese cake. Return to oven for additional 5 minutes. Chill for at least 2 hours prior to serving.

Giorgio's Table

Giorgio and Elisabetta Paradisi took a gamble in 1995 when they opened Giorgio's Table, an Italian restaurant on Virgin Gorda. They were offered a location on-site at an established resort. As the only Italian restaurant on Virgin Gorda, they would have no direct competition. So where was the gamble? Well, not only have neither Giorgio nor Betty ever operated or worked in an Italian restaurant, neither have ever worked in the restaurant business at all.

Amazingly, this little detail did not deter them in the least. "But we have taste," says Betty. "And we are not stupid people," adds Giorgio. Perhaps it is their lack of experience and nonchalance that has allowed them the freedom to develop a fresh approach to Italian cuisine. With the help of Chef Tridick Peters, of St. Vincent, Giorgio established a menu that blended Italian and Caribbean flavors. Many of the ingredients are Italian, which are flown into St. Martin and shipped up to Virgin Gorda, and some of the recipes are traditional. However, Giorgio explains that the menu is "...not classic Italian, but creative Italian. It is Italian with the soul of the Caribbean." Obviously there aren't many purists in our midst, as Giorgio's has been a hit since the day it opened.

One feature of the menu that is all Italian is the wine list. Giorgio's carries only Italian wines and the list includes an impressive one hundred and fifty varieties. Connoisseurs are startled and delighted to find such rare choices on such a small island.

The dining room, with tables beautifully set with Italian linens and hand-painted dinnerware, looks out over the Channel. The atmosphere is one of simple elegance.

The view of Mahoe and Pond Bays is just the beginning of this experience. Wait until you taste the food!

Harbour View

Mike and Dorothea Fisher left their home in Ohio and hit the high seas in 1984. They sailed their boat Aeolus around the world for six years, stopping to work in the restaurant business in various places along the way. The pair settled in BVI waters in 1990 and ran a charter boat there for the next ten years, where they wined and dined their guests. Three years ago, it was finally time for something different. Mike and Dorothea came ashore on Tortola, bought an empty shell of a building, and built themselves a restaurant. They named it Harbour View for it's magnificent view of Fat Hog Bay.

Harbour View is best known for good food, good service, and a relaxed, unpretentious atmosphere. Dorothea has developed a menu that specializes in seafood and pasta, but also includes pizza that many customers return for. The clientele consists of about a fifty-fifty split of locals and visitors, with most being return customers from both camps.

Open for lunch and dinner, Mike and Dorothea concentrate on the restaurant business rather than the tourist trade. They tried live local music for a while, but decided to come back and concentrate on their basic product — good food and drink. There is little advertisement, no ploys such as T-shirts or souvenirs, and no special menus during tourist season. They believe that if the product is good, the people will come. "We sell good food and drink year round," says Mike firmly. Can't argue with that.

Grouper Florentine
(serves 4)

4 servings grouper
1 cup heavy cream
1/4 cup white wine
2 cups fresh spinach
1/4 cup grated parmesan cheese
juice of 1/2 lemon
butter
flour
salt and pepper

Salt and pepper the grouper then dust with flour. Sauté with butter, 3 minutes per side then add white wine, heavy cream and lemon juice. Reduce by 1/2 then add spinach and top with parmesan.

Stuffed Artichoke Hearts
(serves 4)

1 can artchoke hearts	capers
4 oz. smoked salmon	onions
4 tbsp. cream cheese	

Open artichoke hearts. Stuff with cream cheese and smoked salmon. Top with onions and capers. Bake in oven at 350 degees for 15 minutes.

. . . .

East Ender (drink)

3 oz. Mt. Gay rum	1/2 oz. cointreau
2 oz. banana liquer	1 oz. orange juice
1/2 oz. lime juice	

Don't drink too many of these.

The Jolly Roger
INN & RESTAURANT

Skulls and crossbones, rum drinks, music and revelry on the shoreline — these are all things that you would expect from an establishment named The Jolly Roger Inn and Restaurant, and you will not be disappointed. You might also be very surprised at the quality of food served. No pirate who came ashore here in the past ever had it so good. You won't be surprised for long, however; only until you learn that owner, Lou, is a restaurateur from way back. He owned a famous rib joint in Queens until recently, when he sold it to concentrate his know-how on the Jolly Roger.

Chef Scott Weston describes the menu as an accumulation of recipes from the chefs of past and present.

There is an emphasis on fish, which local fishermen deliver fresh to the onsite dock, but there is also a wide assortment of dishes, from Caribbean to Thai. Scott, who comes from a varied background, started in Iowa, cooked his way to Colorado and Martha's Vineyard, and then onto the USVI. He especially likes to cook traditional Mexican and Italian foods.

The Jolly Roger is closely associated with the sailing community, hosting the West End Regatta, called the Sweetheart Regatta. It is also home to the very prestigious Loyal West End Yacht Club. You can find out more from the members there - over a few Jolly Roger cocktails.

Sweet Soy and Saki Marinated Sea Bass with Wilted Bok Choy and Pickled Ginger

6 8-oz. sea bass fillets, skinned
2 cups soy sauce
1/2 cup peanut oil
1/2 cup raw sugar (brown can be substituted)
2 cups Saki
1 head bok choy, coarsely chopped
2 oz. rice wine vinegar

Combine soy, oil, sugar and Saki and mix well. Marinate fish in refrigerator up to one hour before serving.

Preheat broiler. Place marinated bass fillets on flat baking sheet and place on top rack of broiler. Remove when fish is opaque and flakes easily

Heat up wok or pan large enough to hold bok choy. Place all of the cabbage in wok, add rice vinegar, cover and remove from heat immediately, tossing once to wilt cabbage.

Cover plate with layer of jasmine or other white rice. Place fillet on rice, top with wilted cabbage and pickled ginger. Serve with wasabi.

Nori Wrapped Tempura Tuna with Asian Slaw

1 lb. fresh yellowfin or ahi tuna, cut into one-inch square strips
Nori sheets 4-5
tempura mix
sesame oil

Asian Slaw:
Napa cabbage, one head finely shredded
1 cup black vinegar
1/2 cup soy sauce
2 cups sesame oil
1 tbsp. dried wasabi powder
2 scallions, finely chopped

Lay tuna along short side of nori paper covering from end to end. Roll nori around tuna until wrapped completely. Add another layer of tuna and roll until nori is completely used. Refrigerate while remaining tuna is rolled.

Heat enough sesame oil in wok or deep pan to cover rolls. Prepare tempura batter according to directions. Lightly flour tuna roll and pat off excess flour. Dip roll into tempura and fry at 350 until batter is slightly brown. Remove from heat source and slice into 8 pieces.

Prepare dressing by combining all ingredients except scallions and cabbage in blender and blend until smooth and a cream-like consistancy appears. Toss cabbage and scallions in dressing and place on a chilled plate. Arrange tuna slices on bed of slaw. Serve with pickled ginger and prepared wasabi.

Le Cabanon

The clientele at Le Cabanon, in the center of Road Town, falls into three main categories: tourists who want a change from Caribbean fare, residents who need the change, and those who love French dining no matter where they are or for how long. At Le Cabanon it is French all the way. The two owners, who serve as the chefs along with a third chef, are Parisian. The menu is strictly French cuisine, with the products and raw supplies in the kitchen flown in weekly from France.

Owners Christophe Buisgiraid, Sebastian Liegeard, and the third chef, Walter Faynel, place a high priority on authenticity. A common problem experienced and lamented in restaurants throughout the BVI is the timely availability of fresh supplies from across the channel. Now, imagine importing your goods from across the Atlantic. They believe the effort is worth it. The customers agree as they partake of such rarities as escargot, turbot, or rabbit.

It is word-of-mouth that brings the patrons. This is the only French restaurant in the Territory, and so word traveled fast when the doors were opened four years ago. On any given day or night the informal open-air eatery is full of diners. When you visit, you might find Sebastian and Walter in the kitchen, while Christophe is taking care of the front of the house.

Marjoram Turbo Fillet with Chive Mash Potatoes
(serves 6)

1 turbot, 2.5-3 kg. in weight
250 gms. butter
250 ml. of heavy (double) cream
1 kg. potatoes
1/2 bunch of fresh marjoram
1 bunch of chives
olive oil, salt and freshly milled pepper

For the sauce:
Fillet and de-bone the turbot and remove the skin. Reserve the fillets. Soak the fish bones, head and skin in cold water for about 1 hour, and then rinse thoroughly. Place the fish bones, head and skin in a saucepan and cover to approximately twice its volume with water. Simmer, without boiling for 45 minutes. Pour the liquid through a sieve into a second saucepan and return to the heat. Reduce the liquid until there is just 15 cl left. In the meantime, wash and shred the marjoram. Slowly add 5 cl of the cream to the sauce and mix well. Add 150 gms of the butter in little pieces to the sauce whilst stirring. When the butter has melted, add the shredded marjoram.

Preparing the Turbot:
The turbot has four fillets, two of them considerably larger. Cut the larger two in half so you have six fillets of equal size. Heat a pan, add the oil and when very hot, sear the fish on one side for 15 seconds. Turn the fish over, add a small amount of butter to the pan, lower the heat and cook for a further 45 seconds. Do not exceed this time.

For the Chive Mashed Potatoes:
Peel, wash and chop the potatoes into chunks. Finely chop the chives. Put the potato pieces in salted water and bring to a boil. When the potatoes are soft enough to run a knife through without resistance, remove from the heat and drain. Mash the potatoes with 20 cl of cream and about 100 gms of butter. Season to taste, add most of the chives (reserving the rest for decoration) and continue mashing until well mixed.
Place two spoons of potatoes on each plate. Using a large spoon, fashion the potatoes into a flat-topped oval. Place the turbot fillet on top. Pour the sauce over the fillets and sprinkle with the remainder of the chives to serve.

Duck Breast Tournedos with Porcini (cap)
Mushroom Stuffing
(serves 6)

1 kg. of duck breast fillets, skin removed
300 g. of porcini/caps (not dried)
6 shallots
150 ml. of cognac
100 ml. of demi-glace sauce
100 ml. of heavy (double) cream
150 g. of butter
You will also need string suitable for cooking, olive oil, salt and freshly milled pepper.

For the Porcini Stuffing:
Rinse the mushrooms thoroughly and slice them thinly. Slice the shallots into very fine pieces. Using 50 g. of the butter, sear the mushrooms and shallots on a low heat with salt and pepper to taste for about 15 minutes (until soft but not charred). Deglaze the pan with the cognac and allow the liquid to reduce until the mushroom mixture is almost dry. Reserve half of this for the stuffing.

For the Porcini Sauce:
Place half of the mushroom and shallot mixture in a saucepan. Add the cream and demi-glace sauce, and salt and pepper to taste and bring to a boil. As soon as the mixture starts to bubble, add the remainder of the butter and stir vigorously until all the butter has melted. Remove from the heat and pour into a ceramic bowl. The sauce should then be kept hot by placing in a bain-marie until ready for use.

Preparing the Duck Tournedos:
Divide the mushroom stuffing into six equal parts. Using a kitchen hammer, flatten the duck fillets until about 2.25 cms wide. It is wise to remove the central nerve out of the fillet at this stage. Join 4-5 of the fillets lengthwise, with an overlap of approximately 1.5 cm. Spread the stuffing centrally along the length of each tournedos, and season to taste. Carefully roll each tournedos (short side) from right to left and tie securely with kitchen string. Sear the tournedos in very hot olive oil for two to three minutes on each side. Place the tournedos, one per person on plates and remove the string. Pour the sauce over the top and decorate with chervil.

The Last Resort

The Last Resort, first conceived by Tony and Jackie Snell in 1970, has appeared consistently on the "to do" list of visitors in the BVI for the past thirty years. So what's the draw? Well, for some, it's been the resort animals: the parrots, dogs, and donkeys, the most famous being Chocolate, the late beer-drinking donkey. The animals have always been as popular with the guests as any of the humans on the island. That's saying something, as everyone loved Jackie and the larger-than-life Tony. Jackie was the driving force behind the development of the resort, while Tony was the front man, entertaining the crowds and bringing them back year after year. In years past, many guests also came for the roast beef buffet.

These days the tiny island in the middle of Trellis Bay is under the management of Ben Banford, and it is thriving. There are still the animals (the present donkey, Vanilla, is a teetotaller), and the characters (the head chef is also the entertainer), but there has been a significant change in the food. The buffet has been replaced by a much more ambitious menu executed by Alistair Broderick and John Aldridge. Out with the Baron of Beef and in with such exotic selections as Alligator Thai Curry. "People still radio in sometimes to make reservations for the buffet and sound a bit disappointed to hear that it is gone," says Ben, "but they generally come away happy, pleasantly surprised by the changes."

Ben and Alistair are both young, but by no means are they novices. They have honed their skills in places such as Brighton, the famous resort town in England. Alistair was also once private chef to a well-known Russian mafia figure. He worked the kitchen under the watch of machine-gun-toting security. Though a slower, more secure existence was a drawing point for the two partners and their families, it took a fair amount of courage to take on the Last Resort.

Al, the singing chef, starts his set once all have been fed. It is worth the wait and even Vanilla the donkey will pop his head in to check it out.

Roast Asian Spiced Duck with Orange and Anise Butter Sauce
(serves 4)

4 fresh duck breasts
1 ltr. orange juice
6 star anise pods
1 pack dry chow mein noodles
chopped ginger, onion and garlic
vegetables for stir fry:
    mange tout, shredded bok choy, carrots, peppers,
    yellow squash
5 spice powder
3 tbsp. oyster sauce
2 tbsp. soy sauce
3 tbsp. sherry
1 250 gm. pack butter
1 bunch cilantro or coriander, dependant on your
geographic preference
salt and pepper

For the duck:
Score the fat, salt and dust with 5 spice powder. Leave
for 1 hour to rest in the fridge. Place the duck, skin side
down, in a hot dry pan, sear until brown then flip and
place in a hot oven for 3-4 minutes. Make sure not to
overcook — the duck should be served pink. Leave to
rest for a minute then slice and serve on top of the noo-
dle chow mein.

For the orange sauce:
Reduce the juice with the star anise until there is about
1/2 of the liquid remaining—this will take about 15 mins.
While the duck is resting, cube the butter and whisk
into the orange reduction over a medium heat. Add salt
and pepper and some chopped cilantro.

For the noodles:
Boil enough water in a pan to submerse the noodles.
Remove pan from the heat and leave the noodles to
absorb for 5 minutes, then strain and cool. In a wok,
heat sesame oil until smoking. Add onions, ginger,
garlic and a little 5 spice powder. Add vegetables. Stir
fry for 3 minutes. Add the sherry and deglaze, then add
soy sauce, oyster sauce and a little of the orange
reduction. Finally, add the noodles, salt and pepper
and some chopped cilantro.

To serve, pile the chow mein onto the plate, lay the
sliced duck on top, and spoon the sauce around.
Garnish with cilantro sprigs or deep-fried leaves of
bok choy.

. . . .

Steak Rossini
(serves 4)

This dish was created by the chef to the famous Italian
composer. A delicious alternative to a classic pepper
sauce.

4 8-oz. fillet steaks (tenderloin/mignon)
1/2 lb. mushrooms
1/2 cup brandy
1 tbsp. English mustard
1 tbsp. whole grain mustard
2 tbsp. chicken liver patè
2 cups stock or demi glace
1 cup cream
sliced bread for croutes
oil and chopped mixed herbs
salt and pepper

For the croutes:
Cut 4 circles from the bread (big enough for the steaks
to sit on), douse with oil, sprinkle with herbs and season with salt and pepper. Place on a tray in a hot oven
and cook until golden. When you are ready to serve,
spread the croutes with a thin layer of patè and place
under the steaks.

For the steak:
Char grill or pan fry to your liking.

For the sauce:
Heat a medium size frying pan and add butter and
sliced mushrooms. Fry until golden, then pour in
brandy and allow to flame. When the flaming stops
add patè, mustards, stock and cream. Allow to boil, stir
and reduce to favoured consistency.

To serve, place the steaks on the croutes and pour over
the sauce, accompany with your favorite combination
of vegetables and potatoes.

55

Little Dix Bay

Laurence Rockefeller built Little Dix Bay in 1961. In creating the ultimate retreat, he chose Virgin Gorda, a lesser known island of the then seldom-traveled British Virgin Islands. Though ownership has changed over the last forty years, the lasting keyword is exclusivity.

The current executive chef is Denis Jaricot. It is no coincidence that he is here, but his route was anything but direct. Except for a grandfather who had a deli in Lyons where he grew up, Denis' family background did not indicate a future in food. However, he was interested in cooking as far back as he can remember. After training in Paris and experience at such prominent hotels as Four Seasons and Intercontinental, Denis landed at the Cuisine Art Resort in Anguilla. There he was recruited by the current Little Dix Bay GM.

Managing some of the top kitchens in the western world has provided Denis with more than the obvious culinary skills. He also brings to his new post experience in two very current food and beverage areas of focus - dietary concerns and hydroponics. Both are featured in his long-range plans for Little Dix Bay.

His most immediate concentration, since his arrival in December, has been in extending quality variety to the three on-site restaurants. The beach grill (Little Dix Bay's concession to hamburgers and hotdogs) has been up-graded to fresh grouper wraps and Mediterranean salads. Pasta nights and cultural food tasting spice up the Sugar Mill, which covers the middle ground with its steak and fish cuisine. The formal dining room offers a Caribbean/Mediterranean cuisine that promotes experimentation, while preserving the traditions of fine dining.

As his first season winds down, Denis can start implementing his bigger ideas. His goal is to reach the stars —five of them.

Mad Dog

Mad Dog is a little bar near the Baths on Virgin Gorda. Built in the tradition of the Caribbean shuttered cottage, set amongst boulders, green lawns, flowering shrubs, and steady breezes, the bar is a favorite getaway. Tourists trudging up from the Baths, windjammer passengers looking for a friendly onshore stop, and local residents seeking a cool break after a hot day all make their way to Mad Dog.

There, they are greeted and taken care of by Edith Davis: bartender, cook, tour guide, confidante, mother, and the recognized Piña Colada Queen of the BVI. One will also find Edith's sidekick, Lilia Eugene.

Built in 1989 by American Steve Green and Englishman Colin McCullough, Mad Dog is a daytime bar, open from nine am to seven pm. It is not a restaurant. The menu, from day one, has offered hotdogs and sandwiches. Period. Strangely enough, this grabs people

and it is not unusual to hear a returning customer order a "crab sandwich like the one I had here two years ago" or "one of your BLT's please" as if it were a gourmet meal. For some reason the food just works.

There is a bit of hustle-bustle now and then when a function is held on the premises— it is ideal for a party, be it a wedding reception or fund-raiser. Generally, though, Mad Dog is a quiet oasis. Visitors sit back on the shady deck or recline in the hammock, sip their drinks, grab a bite, and soak up the peace and quiet.

Mad Dog caps and T-shirts are on sale and have become a tradition. The design, while always featuring the cartoon mad dog, changes each year. Many returning guests update their wardrobes annually with a memento from the bar.

Mama Rita's
FINISH LINE CAFÉ

When looking for the restaurant that serves the best Italian food in town, whether in Rome, New York, or the BVI, you won't find it in the middle of the tourist district. It will be off the beaten track. So, in getting help to find it, you can't ask at the tourist office or your hotel desk. One must ask the locals, specifically the local restaurateurs. In the BVI that means being directed to Mama Rita's Finish Line Café in Sea Cow Bay, Tortola, known locally as Rita's. You'll know that you're in the right place when you find that it's not located on a picturesque waterfront property and it is full of local clientele, many of them from the food trade.

This is just the way Rita wants it. "I don't advertise. I want them to come for my food. First my friends came and they sent others." An unorthodox formula in a town that trades on the tourist dollar, but one that seems to work for Rita.

At the Finish Line Café you can choose from northern or southern Italian dishes or West Indian. With a surname like Cavallo, it comes as no surprise to learn that Rita's knowledge of Italian cuisine was not so much learned as absorbed into her bloodstream during her childhood in New Jersey. In the twelve years that she has lived here in the BVI, Rita has also become adept at local dishes and makes a mean goat water.

Pasta Alfredo With Vegetables, Shrimp or Chicken

1 tbsp. butter
2 tbsp. cream sherry
6 oz. chicken breast or 8 shrimp
4 broccoli flowers
6 cut and blanched carrots sliced in strips
1 cup heavy cream
1/4 tsp. grated fresh nutmeg
1/4 lb. cooked pasta of choice
1/2 cup parmesan cheese

Sauté the chicken or shrimp in butter. Add the cream, broccoli, carrots and nutmeg and let simmer. Add the pasta and warm it well. Add the parmesan cheese and serve.

. . . .

Mussels in Broth Over Pasta

1/4 cup extra virgin olive oil
1/4 cup chopped leeks
1/4 cup chopped shallots
1/4 cup chopped sweet onion
1 quart clam juice
pinch of salt
pinch of cayenne pepper
pinch of white pepper
1/4 cup chopped fresh parsley
1/4 cup chopped fresh basil
60 mussels cleaned
2 cloves of chopped garlic

Sauté the onions, shallots, garlic and leeks in the olive oil until soft. Add all seasonings and the clam juice and bring to a boil. Lower the heat and add the mussels and slowly bring back to a boil. Serve over capelinni or other pasta.

Yellowfin Tuna Over Salad

Marinate tuna in the following:
  1 tbsp. sesame oil
  2 tbsp. grated fresh ginger
  1/2 tsp. grated fresh garlic
  1 tbsp. thinly sliced leek
  1 tbsp. thinly sliced shallot

Pan sear tuna and place over a salad of lettuce, radicchio, cucumber, red onion and plum tomato.

Dress the salad with extra virgin olive oil, balsamic vinegar, granulated garlic, salt, white pepper, basil and a pinch of sugar.

You just have to meet Rita!!! The Finish Line Café is difficult to find, even if you ask. Ask instead for Rita's. All the locals know where she is. She alone is worth the effort and the food is great to boot.

Mine Shaft

In the competitive world of the bar and restaurant business you need a hook. The Mineshaft in Virgin Gorda has several.

The most obvious is its association with the Copper Mine National Park. Located on the side of the hill just at the edge of the park, the restaurant catches the tourists who visit the historic ruins. Its name and motif skillfully plays on the connection, with mining tools, miner's helmets, and a bucket containing the secret ingredients of the famous "Cave-in" drink that gets lowered from a pulley.

Another hook is the food. It's good, very good: for example the mouthwatering coconut curried shrimp. It is also varied, with dishes ranging from taco salad to the best BBQ ribs on Virgin Gorda. Finally, the prices are inexpensive, only seven to twenty-five dollars a plate. The Mine Shaft's weekly food fests include Tuesday night BBQ buffet and Sunday brunch.

The restaurant's most powerful hook is personality, which the two owners, brothers Elton and Lincoln Sprauve, are dripping with. They are the ultimate hosts: funny, chatty, always laughing and entertaining, and their clientele love them. Experience is also important, and the brothers have worked, between them, in every major resort on the island.

The final hook is one the brothers cannot take credit for. Perched on a hilltop overlooking both the Atlantic and the Caribbean, the Mine Shaft offers its customers the most exquisite sunsets that can be had. Seasoned travelers, who have sampled sunsets worldwide, are entranced. Diners come early to see the show and they return year after year, with friends, to share the magic.

Mine Shaft Curried Coconut Shrimp

24 shrimp
6 tsp. curry powder
1 cup diced red, green and yellow peppers
1/2 cup diced white onions
garlic
olive oil

Cook together in a large fry pan and add Bacardi Limon rum and Coco Lopez to taste. Serve with rice.

. . . .

Blackened Grouper and Seasoned Rice

Dredge fish in blackening seasoning and fry in hot olive oil, turning only once.

Seasoned rice
Add chopped yellow, green and red peppers to black beans. Cook with basil, parsley, 2 bay leafs and Season-All.

Crab Fritters

In a food processor blend red, yellow and green peppers, red and white onions, garlic, parsley, black pepper and crabmeat.

Add baking powder and continue to add flour until a spoon can stand up in it.

Drop from a spoon into hot oil and serve with sauce of choice.

Mrs. Scatliffe's
RESTAURANT & BAR

Born and brought up on Tortola, Mrs. Scatliffe spent many of her seventy-five years cooking in other people's restaurants, such as Sebastian's and Sugar Mill. Then, twenty years ago, at an age when most would be thinking of retirement, she opened Mrs. Scatliffe's Restaurant and Bar in Carrot Bay on Tortola's north shore. There she offers her guests true, unadulterated local cuisine. Mrs. Scatliffe doesn't just "do" local, she's the real article.

You want authentic Caribbean? How about a soursop daiquiri followed by fungi or curried goat? Maybe some papaya or breadfruit soup with hot dumbread? Oldwife or triggerfish in an onion and tomato sauce? Perhaps coconut chicken with rice served in a coconut shell? What may be old-style cooking to Mrs. Scatliffe is exotica for her foreign guests.

She grows her own fruit (mango, papaya, and banana) in her garden, raises her own goats, and cooks all of her own food with the help of her daughter. Each meal is prepared for the particular diners of that evening. You must call ahead with your reservation and choice of main course.

Mrs. Scatliffe has both witnessed and played a role in the birth of tourism in the BVI. On the topic of the ups and downs of the restaurant business, she shrugs and says, "Every day is fishin' day but not every day is catchin' day." In "fishin" for excellent local cooking, a trip to Mrs. Scatliffe's is definitely a "catchin" day.

Curried Goat

Boil several pounds of goat meat on the bone until it is easy to de-bone. Trim all fat and gristle and put back in pot. Add onion, garlic, celery, thyme, raisins, salt and pepper, shredded coconut, curry and a ripe banana. Do not add carrots or cabbage or it will be like everyone else's stew. Simmer until tender.

. . . .

Chicken and Coconut with Rice

Boil the chicken with carrots, celery, onions, and salt and pepper. When 3/4 done remove chicken and cut off the bone into cubes. Add flour to thicken and put the chicken back. Grate a coconut into water. Squeeze the water out into the pot. Add a handful of grated coconut and finish cooking. Serve in a coconut shell over rice.

Papaya Soup

Go to the nearest papaya tree and pick one that is turning yellow but is still hard. The seeds must be black. Peel, chop and wash the papaya. Add to a pot of water with onion, thyme, celery, and garlic. Salt and pepper to taste. Boil until smooth. (I think she used a blender or food processor to make it creamy.)

Neptune's Treasure

The Soares family came from Bermuda to Anegada forty years ago to commercially fish the BVI waters. The seeds of the restaurant branch of the business were sown a few years later when Mom, who was home on the beach with the daughters while Dad and the sons went fishing, began cooking and selling pizza out of their home. Demand grew and the family restaurant, Neptune's Treasure, was born.

Both the restaurant and the fish business flourished. With the girls helping Mom in the restaurant and the boys on the boat with Dad, the second generation was groomed to take over.

Today, sons Mark and Dean along with nephew Alan and son-in-law Randy Thielman, now run the boat,

Argus. Their fish is served in top restaurants throughout the BVI and is identified on menus as "Soares" catch as a guarantee of quality.

Daughter, Linda Soares-Thielman, assumed command of Neptune's Treasure six years ago, and it too has prospered in her capable hands. Linda's expertise in the kitchen is a culmination of her years of internship with Julie (Mom) along with the addition of a few of her own tastes and twists. Her specialty is fish, naturally, and her style is a mixture of Bermudian and Caribbean with a dash of Portuguese. Building on her mother's motto of "Never serve to other's what you wouldn't want to eat yourself," Linda strives for excellence with every dish.

Fish Fingers
(serves 2)

Cut fish in finger-size pieces. (16 fingers). Place in bowl. Season with salt, pepper, and Caribbean jerk seasoning. Add milk to cover fingers. Let marinate for 2 hours. Then roll fingers in flour. Deep fry in very hot oil until golden brown. Remove and drain on paper towels. Serve while hot along with cocktail sauce of your choice.

. . . .

Neptune's Treasure's Famous Cole Slaw

Shred one green cabbage. Peel and grate one jumbo carrot. Add a few shakes of dried parsley flakes. Mix well.

Sauce:
mayonnaise (approximately 3 cups)
cider vinegar to taste
sugar to taste

Whisk until smooth. Add to cabbage mix. Cover and chill until ready to serve.

Broiled Sword Fish

2 swordfish steaks

Line shallow pan with foil. Spray with non-stick cooking spray. Pour lemon juice in pan, just enough to cover bottom. Add swordfish steaks. Spread margarine or butter on top of the steaks. Lightly sprinkle seasoning of your choice and paprika. Let marinate for approximately 2 hours in chiller.

Heat broiler. Pour off lemon juice except for about 2 tablespoons. Place pan with sword steaks in oven and broil for about 7-9 minutes (depending upon the thickness of the steaks). When cooked, pour sauce over fish. Garnish with fresh lemon twist and fresh parsley sprig and serve.

North Shore Shell Museum

BAR & RESTAURANT

The North Shore Shell Museum Bar & Restaurant is quite a mouthful, but it is "all that." When you walk in the door you are a bit overwhelmed by the array of artifacts that surround you: hand painted signs displaying nuggets of local wisdom in the vernacular, all manner of shells from nearby beaches, and traditional musical instruments displayed invitingly. You instantly know that you have found something special.

Egberth and Mona Donovan are devoted to the family crusade of preserving island traditions. Mona, not surprisingly, is Mrs. Scatliffe's daughter. The Donovan's campaign is carried over into the kitchen. They raise most of their own produce on the mountain behind their premises and bring it down by donkey. They run their own fishing boat and bake their bread in out-door ovens. The menu is not the typical Caribbean/International venue found in most restaurants. This is pure BVI cooking ,"like we do it in our homes — the old way," says Egberth. Fungi, steamed fish, stewed chicken, dumplings, and johnnycake all find their way onto the menu.

Both tourists and locals congregate at the North Shore restaurant morning, noon, and night. The most popular meal on the menu is breakfast, specifically the Surfer's Breakfast, which consists of bacon, eggs, and coconut or banana pancakes with mango or papaya syrup. The syrup is produced onsite from the fruit of the backyard orchards. Evening meals are followed by musical sessions where one and all are invited to join in with the traditional instruments kept on hand.

The food, music, décor, and practice of bringing local children on nature hunts, are all designed to preserve the BVI heritage in a world of progress.

Grilled Fish

Season fish with any spices, but always use garlic, black pepper and onion. Crush with mortar and coat fish. Grill on open fire. Serve with fungie, roasted bread fruit and boiled banana. Use a green banana and boil the banana with water and a little salt in its skin for 5-6 minutes.

. . . .

Cracked Conch Homemade Style

Mix flour, eggs and breadcrumbs together and coat the conch. Fry in oil. When finished, use a little melted butter and/or lime juice to season it.

Chicken Tortola (Grilled chicken with fruit sauce)

Grill chicken with onion. Boil mango and guava fruits and add chicken. Boil until tender. Serve with fresh garden salad.

At dinner there is fungi band music. The guests are given instruments and they play along after dinner.

Palm's Delight

Iona Dawson, born and bred in Tortola, learned about cooking while working in several restaurants on the island. Tired of working for other people, she decided to set out on her own and opened a snack bar selling ice cream, sandwiches, and carrot cake.

Her son, as adventurous as she, decided to try BBQ to see if it caught on. It did and soon, at the urgings of her customers, Iona began to branch out to include the full-range West Indian menu she carries today at her restaurant, Palm's Delight, in Carrot Bay.

It is quite a family affair with one son on the grill and another in the kitchen with Mum. They all cook strictly Caribbean food: provision, dumplings, johnnycake, and fungi. "Basic food," Iona calls it. She also has

some specialties that she treats her customers to, for example, her fish in garlic Creole sauce.

Though her "basic food" obviously attracts local clientele, she also gets a lot of tourists. Her most famous guest was Peter Jennings. "But I don't remember what he ate," she giggles.

Located literally inches from the shoreline, Palm's Delight has felt the onslaught of a few hurricanes in the past ten years. However, it has weathered them all and lost only the ice cream concession to hurricane Marilyn. These kinds of problems come with owning your own business, but Iona wouldn't go back. "It's a lot harder when you work for yourself, but I love it."

Chicken in Ginger Wine Sauce

Flatten two boneless breasts. Dredge in flour and dip in a beaten egg. Dredge in bread crumbs. Grill with a bit of oil or butter. Boil 1 cup of Stone's Green Ginger Wine and reduce by 1/2. Add some heavy cream and simmer until it thickens. Pour over the chicken and serve with fried plantains, rice and beans, and fungi.

. . . .

Fried Plantains

This is on every West Indian menu and goes well with everything. Fry ripe (yellow and soft) plantains in hot oil for about two minutes, until soft and light brown. Another way to do them is to grill them in their skins until they open. Baste with butter and brown sugar and rum. If you slice and fry them green and serve plain you have tostadas, a Puerto Rican dish.

Fungi

Simply boil some okra and add corn meal, salt and a bit of oil until it thickens. This is the West Indian version of Polenta and some West Indian cooks claim it came over with Columbus.

. . . .

Steamed Fish with Green Bananas and Dumplings

Boil a fresh fish (snapper, oldwife or any white fish) with enough water to cover with peppers, onions and a bit of butter. About 10-15 minutes. Add two green bananas (skin on) to the pot and boil until soft. Reserve most of the water, and add some mayonnaise to 3/4 cup of it. Make the dumplings by kneading together corn meal, salt, water and butter and drop spoonfuls into the fish stock and boil. Pour the mayo sauce over the fish and serve with sweet potatoes.

Pam's Kitchen

You have probably noticed products such as loaves, cookies, jams, and chutneys marked with "Pam's Kitchen" in shops throughout the BVI. So who is this Pam and where is her kitchen that supplies all of these goodies?

Well, the kitchen is a brightly colored little bakery that occupies a corner of the Neptune's Treasure site on Anegada. Pam is Pam Soares, married to the oldest brother of the renowned Anegada family. The idea for her kitchen business hatched during her days as a taxi driver on the island. A common complaint from her passengers concerned the time and expense of traveling to the village for fresh bread. An entrepreneur at heart and a good cook as well, Pam saw the gap and set about filling it. After depositing her passengers at the beach or a restaurant, she would buzz home, bake bread, and have it ready when she picked the passengers up again.

Encouraged by the positive response, Pam began producing more goods such as banana bread, brownies, and chocolate chip cookies. She would load the food, along with her young kids, into a dinghy and go boat-to-boat at the anchorages selling her baked goodies. Unable to keep up with the demand from her home, she eventually built her commercial kitchen and bakery in 1990.

You can visit Pam's Kitchen to sample the goods at their source. In fact I challenge you to try to walk by without succumbing to the smells wafting from the windows and the cozy little deck out front. Go on, just try.

Pam's Kitchen Banana Bread

Combine 2 pounds of bananas
2 cups sugar
1 cup Crisco or butter
1 tsp. baking soda
6 eggs
4 cups flour

Beat for a few minutes and pour into baking pans and bake at 350 degrees for 50-60 minutes

Peg Leg Landing

In its twenty-five year history, Peg Leg Landing has undergone various makeovers in appearance and style as ownership and management have changed. Presently owned by Heather Anderson, the restaurant is more popular than ever. "It's the atmosphere," says head chef, Todd Hill, modestly.

Peg Leg has a pleasing English pub feel — all dark polished wood inside — though without the heavy indoor overtones, thanks to an open plan that exposes the bright blues of sky and water on all sides. Perched, literally, on the breakwater at the entrance of Nanny Cay, it has the waves on one side and the sheltered inner harbour on the other. It has atmosphere, for sure, but it also has great food.

American, French, and Caribbean Fusion is how Todd Hill, master chef at Peg Leg Landing, describes the dishes he prepares. It's a style, he explains, that is inspired by the French-influenced cooking he learned in Switzerland, coloured by the North American approach of his background, and tempered by the availability of fresh Caribbean ingredients.

Peg Leg has long been a hotspot for boat charters. It hosts some of the large annual water sporting affairs such as The BVI Spring Regatta, HiHo windsurfing ceremonies, and KATS events. Such ambitious undertakings require a strong staff base as they cater to huge numbers that are intent on eating and drinking themselves through their successes or defeats. The long-standing staff here is up to the task. "Everyone who works here is willing to do whatever it takes to get the job done," Todd says with pride. It's getting the job done with style that Todd can take a bow for.

Chicken Lepourcelet

2.5 oz. chicken breast, skinless/boneless
8 oz. creme fraiche or 4 oz. sour cream and 4 oz. plain yogurt
2 oz. unsalted butter
3 large mushrooms, sliced
3 strips bacon, diced
1 small onion, sliced
3 cloves garlic
salt and pepper
red wine

Butterfly and lightly season chicken breast with salt and pepper. Pan sear in butter until golden. Remove breast from pan. Add bacon and sautee 2-3 minutes. Add sliced mushrooms and onions with whole crushed cloves of garlic. Sauté until mushrooms and onions are tender. Deglaze with red wine, add creme fraiche. Mix and heat until sauce just starts to boil. Add chicken and heat 1 minute. Serve immediately.

. . . .

Pamesan Herb Encrusted Tuna with Sesame Ginger Aioli

2 6-oz. tuna steaks - preferably yellowfin
6 oz parmesan cheese, grated finely
3 oz. chopped fresh herbs - basil, thyme, parsley and pepper
1 oz. olive oil

Heat olive oil in skillet.
Mix parmesan & fresh herbs.
Coat tuna steaks with parmesan mix, and sear for
   45 seconds per side.
Serve with sesame ginger aioli.

Sesame Ginger Aioli:
4 oz. pickled ginger
1/2 small onion, diced
2 egg yolks
salt and pepper
1 tbsp. sesame oil
1 cup olive oil
1 tbsp. lemon juice
1 tbsp. sesame seeds, toasted

Place pickled ginger, onion, egg yolks, and salt & pepper into food processor. Turn on high & gradually add sesame oil, then olive oil, and last the lemon juice. Serve sauce under tuna and garnish with roasted sesame seeds.

Pusser's

Pusser's may be the only chain of restaurants founded on the back of a bottle of rum. Charles Tobias, the founder of the Pusser's empire, started with the idea of resurrecting the rum disbursed to the sailors of the Royal Navy. Every day these lucky men were given a ration of grog, which consisted of a special West Indian rum and water. When Charles started to make this rum again he called it Pusser's after the purser, the dispenser of the rum. Since that time the brand has been sold to a large distributor and bought back by Tobias.

In addition to the rum, Charles started a line of Pusser's clothing and opened several restaurants. In the BVI there are three Pusser's restaurants. The one in West End or Sopper's Hole is the focal point of a lively village of shops. Here one will find sailors, locals and assorted tourists. It is always lively. The Downtown location, across from the ferry dock, is a favorite of those who work nearby, including many of the staff of other restaurants. The third location is on Marina Cay, a truly breathtaking spot off Great Camanoe Island.

The food at all three is essentially the same. Lest you think that this would breed mediocrity, let me assure you that it is good and sometimes great food. It is a mixture of local i.e. West Indian and pub food. They may have the best burgers in the BVI and the dinner items are outstanding. The locations speak for themselves and the rum is Pusser's.

Pusser's Painkiller

4 parts pineapple juice
1 part cream of coconut
1 part orange juice
Pusser's rum to taste

Serve over ice and grate fresh nutmeg on top and
garnish with fruit.

Coconut Grouper

Fish:
1 8-oz. grouper filet
seasoned flour
tempura beer batter
shredded coconut
peanut oil

Tempura Batter:
1 bottle beer (Budweiser works the best)
1 1/4 cup cake flour
1 tsp. Old Bay Seasoning
1 tsp. sea salt
1 tsp. ground black pepper

Plantain and Citrus Sauce:
2 oz. clarified butter
6 oz. plantain (cut 1" on a bias and pre-cooked)
1/4 cup pineapple chunks (1" cube)
1/4 cup mango chunks (1" cube)
2 oz. white zinfandel wine
2 oz. grapefruit juice
2 oz. orange juice
3 oz. cream (36%)

Heat enough peanut oil in skillet to float the battered filet to 350 degrees. Rinse the grouper filet with cold water and pat dry. Dredge in seasoned flour, shaking off excess flour. Dip filet in batter and then roll it in shredded coconut. Place the filet in heated peanut oil and cook both sides until golden brown.

In a separate skillet heat clarified butter. Place plantain in skillet and sauté until warmed throughout. Add pineapple and mango chunks, heat another 3-4 minutes. Deglaze the skillet with white zinfandel, then add the grapefruit and orange juice. Heat slowly and add cream. Bring to a boil and reduce slightly (approx. 3 minutes).

Pour liquid from pan onto serving plate, place cooked grouper on top of sauce and pour the remainder of skillet contents next to filet, (don't cover grouper with sauce).

To really enhance the presentation, drizzle mango and raspberry puree on plate.

Ginger-Jerked Chicken Breast with Roasted Red Pepper Mashed Potatoes

Marinade:
2 tsp. ground allspice
1/2 tsp. ground nutmeg
1 tsp. kosher salt
2 tsp. dried thyme
1 tsp. ground black pepper
1 tsp. white pepper
2 tbsp. fresh minced ginger
2 tbsp. olive oil
1 tbsp. Pusser's Rum
1 tbsp. fresh lime juice
1 tbsp. brown sugar
1 cup diced red onion
1 cup chopped green onions
4 cloves garlic
1 cup honey
2 habanero peppers

Add above ingredients into food processor and blend until smooth. Divide into 2 equal parts.

Chicken Breasts:
8 boneless, skinless chicken breasts
1/2 marinade from above

Rinse chicken breasts with cold water and pat dry with paper towel. Place chicken breasts into large zip-lock bag and add the marinade, mix well, remove air and place in refrigerator. Allow to marinate for 1 or 2 days. Grill chicken breasts on a hot flame grill. Baste with remaining marinade as desired. Do not use the marinade from the zip-lock bag to grill with.

Roasted Red Pepper Mashed Potatoes: (makes 4 portions)
2 lbs. Idaho baking potatoes (peeled & chunked)
1/2 cup cream (36%)
3/4 cup melted butter
1/2 cup chopped roasted red pepper
1/2 tsp. sea salt
1/4 tsp. ground black pepper

In a large kettle, bring 1 1/2 gallons of water to a boil (enough to cook potatoes in). Add potatoes and cook for approximately 10 minutes or until tender. Drain potatoes. Add cream, butter, roasted red pepper, salt and pepper. Mix until smooth but with some texture.

Rock Café

Paola Moretti always wanted a restaurant, but her dad, a resort owner on Virgin Gorda discouraged her. "Too difficult," he said. However, Paola kept the dream and when she married Dwight Flax, the two set out to make the dream come true. They built the Rock Café.

Italian born, Paola wanted the restaurant to focus on Italian cuisine. Dwight, a BVI native, wanted it to be a disco. They compromised on a sports bar that served Italian food (guess you had to be there). However, that didn't work because it was too noisy for diners and too sedate for sports fans.

The Rock has evolved into a multi-faceted enterprise that has a bit of everything for everyone. A formal inside dining room for formal diners, outside tables among the boulders with a lit waterfall for the more romantic, a piano bar with guest players imported from Europe in the inside modern lounge area, Morris Mark crooning under the stars outside, and a rooftop dance floor for late-night parties. What more could a customer ask for?

The food is Italian, as Paola always envisioned. She trained her chef Eugenie by having him cook alongside her for six months. This year she has brought in another chef, Matteo Puccini, hot off the circuit in Venice. Paola describes the fare as "traditional, not gourmet but not simple, easy to negotiate and easy to eat." The food is, in fact, excellent, plentiful, and affordable.

The Rock Café delivers diversity, wonderful food, talented entertainment, and efficient service. No wonder it is the first restaurant to fill up each night during tourist season and the last to empty during the off-season.

Some would have seen this mass of giant boulders as impossible. Dwight and Paola saw it as an opportunity to create a most unique setting for their restaurant.

Penne Paola

Boil the penne pasta al dente.
Sauce: In a frying pan combine garlic, extra virgin olive oil, whole tomatoes (blended in the food processor before so that the salsa does not have any chunks), salt, and a dash of sugar. Let cook for 20 minutes till the sauce thickens. Still on the fire add a little heavy cream, fresh diced mozzarella and fresh basil. Turn off the fire. Add the pasta and parmesan cheese to your taste.

. . . .

Spaghetti Rock

Boil spaghetti al dente.
Sauce: In a frying pan cook bacon until crispy, drain excess fat, and mince. Add sweet peas, one cup heavy cream, black pepper, little beef broth (fast and easy) and let it cook till desire texture. Add spaghetti and top with parmesan cheese.

Swordfish Sicilian Style

Grill the swordfish to taste (do not overcook).
Sauce: Black olives, fresh diced tomatoes, extra virgin olive oil, garlic, white wine vinegar. Combine all ingredients in a pan and cook for 15 minutes. At the end (turn off the fire) add a good bit of minced fresh Italian parsley and more fresh garlic. Stir and pour on the grilled fish. Nice side dish: boiled white potatoes simply diced and dressed with salt, extra virgin olive oil and fresh parsley.

Roti Palace

Jean Leonard left Trinidad thirty-four years ago, a young girl in search of personal happiness and professional success. She found both in the BVI. Happily married with three children, she is the very successful owner and operator of Roti Palace in Road Town.

For the past sixteen years tourists have sought and found the little restaurant, tucked away on a little side road just above Main Street, lured there by the promise of the BVI's best roti.

So what makes Miss Jean's roti so special? Miss Jean's not saying. She volunteers that part of the secret is in the freshness of every component - from shell to chickpeas to filling - but the actual recipe is a well-guarded secret.

Her customers don't mind as long as they can enjoy the final product. Some prefer the traditional chicken or beef roti; those with more daring palates sample the conch, lobster or whelk. All go for Miss Jean's homemade green mango chutney on the side.

Roti Palace is not at all extravagant. It is bright, cheery, and charming in its simplicity. The unpretentious décor, the friendly atmosphere, and the quality and good name of the product are what make this business one of the longer enduring establishments in the islands.

Royal British Virgin Island Yacht Club

Contrary to its rather austere name and the visions of navy blazers and white gloves that it invokes, the Royal Virgin Island Yacht Club is about as unassuming as it gets. The setting is humble, though the view of Sir Francis Drake Channel from the deck is anything but, the atmosphere friendly, and Susie, the one-woman band who runs the show, has the most casual approach to cooking you will find.

Susie Bowler, a British chef, is the antithesis of the stereotypes of either "stuffy Brit" or "Prima Dona chef." When asked what will be on the menu for tonight, for example, she replies along the lines of, "Oh, I'm not sure yet" or "Well, I'll see what I've got back there and make it up as I go along." But don't

be fooled into thinking that the fare is a slapdash substandard meal that you could have stayed home and whipped up yourself. Susie is an exceptional cook and doesn't disappoint. There are some fixed standards, of course, such as the popular smoked marlin but generally the menu is a reflection of Susie's flair and adaptability.

Susie is like a personal chef to many of her regular guests; she knows what they want and just how they want it. Her relaxed attitude contributes to the general feeling of warmth that greets non-club members and welcomes them into the friendly fold. While members get a break on their bill, non-members are still made to feel as at home as the regulars.

Susie can brighten anyone's day and that is even before you eat.

Roasted Garlic, a Creamy Goat's Cheese Concoction & Crusty Bread
(serves 4)

8 heads of garlic	4 oz. soft goat cheese
1 cup olive oil	1/4 cup heavy cream
4 sprigs of fresh thyme	good bread
1/2 tsp. Caribbean	
Seasoning (or 1/2 tsp. each	
salt and black pepper)	

Heat oven to 400 degrees. Cut each head of garlic in half crosswise. Place garlic halves, cut side up, in a roasting dish large enough to hold all the garlic in one layer. Pour olive oil over the garlic being careful to moisten cut sides. Sprinkle with 1/4 teaspoon of Caribben Seasoning or with salt and black pepper. Strip leaves from thyme and sprinkle over garlic. Cover with foil and roast in oven until tender, which takes about 1 hour. While garlic is roasting, allow goat cheese to soften at room temperature (our rooms being so warm here, this doesn't take long). Using a fork, cream together the goat cheese, heavy cream and the other 1/4 teaspoon of Caribbean Seasoning (or a little sea salt and black pepper). When garlic is ready, allow to cool for about 10 minutes. For each serving, place two halves of garlic from the root end of the bulb, cut sides up on a plate. Beside these put 1/4 of the goat cheese and the bread. Drizzle a little of the roasted garlic flavoured oil over the goat cheese.

(The top half of the garlic bulbs fall apart. Squeeze the garlic from these and use the pulp and any remaining garlic oil for another purpose.)

. . . .

Spinach & Coconut Soup

2 medium onions
1 finely chopped garlic clove
2 oz. unsalted butter
1 large Idaho potato
2 cups chicken or vegetable stock
1 10-oz. bag of pre-washed baby spinach
2 cans coconut milk, well stirred
2 tbsp. shredded coconut, toasted
Caribbean Seasoning (or salt, pepper and a pinch of ground nutmeg)

Finely slice the onions. Melt the butter and stir in the onions and garlic till all buttery. Turn down the heat and press a piece of foil directly onto the onions. Cover pot and cook onions for a long while, 30 minutes or so, stirring occasionally till very tender. Onions should begin to caramelize and can be cut with the side of a wooden spoon. Peel and thinly slice the potato and add to the onions together with the stock. Bring to a boil, cover, turn down heat and cook till potato is very tender. Add the spinach and cook till wilted which will only take a few minutes. Remove from heat, stir in coconut milk and allow to cool for 10 minutes. Purée in a blender, taste and adjust seasoning. Reheat gently to almost, but not quite, boiling and serve sprinkled with toasted coconut.

. . . .

Pasta Shells Tossed with Locally Smoked Marlin in a Creamy Sauce with a Twist of Lemon
(serves 4)

12 oz. dried pasta shells
1 quart heavy cream
4 oz. unsalted butter
1 cup grated parmesan cheese plus 2 tablespoons
8 oz. smoked marlin
zest and juice of 1 lemon
Caribbean Seasoning (or salt and pepper)
1/2 cup finely chopped parsley

Cook the pasta according to the instructions on the packet to al dente (tender but with some bite). Whilst the pasta is cooking make the sauce. Place the cream, butter and parmesan cheese in a large pot and bring to a boil over high heat. Turn the heat down to medium/low and simmer until the sauce thickens enough to coat the back of a spoon. Finely grate the lemon zest and stir into the sauce together with the juice of the lemon. When the pasta is al dente drain and stir into the sauce. Flake the smoked marlin and fold in. Taste and season. Divide between 4 warmed pasta bowls, sprinkle with remaining parmesan and with parsley.

Note: The Caribbean Seasoning I use is available nationwide (!) and is produced by the British Virgin Islands Spice Company from salt harvested from Salt Island. It is an excellent all purpose seasoning.

Saba Rock
ISLAND RESORT

Saba Rock Island Resort's hotel rooms, lovely gardens, and large restaurant cover the entire island of Saba Rock. It is a relatively new resort, but GM David Brick has lost no time in making a mark amongst the older long-established names in the North Sound. The restaurant, noted for its fine food and efficient service, is definitely the new "in" place.

Executive Chef Jeremiah Smith, only 28 years old, has an extensive history in food and beverage. During his high-school years in Kittery, Maine, summers were spent working in his sister's restaurant in Alaska, while school year afternoons were in the kitchen of a local Italian restaurant that he later bought. Jeremiah decided to get serious and studied for three and a half years at Johnson and Wales in Charleston. His introduction to the BVI came through a position as chef with Pusser's in Tortola. Following this post and

a stint as an aviation caterer on private jets, Jeremiah was recruited by David Brick to come to Saba Rock and revamp the menu.

"Basically we have three menus," Jeremiah explains, "the bar menu features more seafood snacks, such as oysters and shrimp, than are found on most BVI bar menus. The "plated" menu out of the kitchen includes such entrees as Tropical Chicken, Dijon Lamb, and Red Snapper with Mango Coulis." However, it is with the buffet that Jeremiah can be the most creative, changing the menu often as he experiments.

A polished menu, cultivated grounds, catchy fish aquarium, and piña coladas that have been coined second best in the BVI, beaten only by Edith's at the Mad Dog... not bad for a new kid on the block.

Tropical Chicken

6 8-oz. chicken breasts

Stuffing:
1/2 cup bread crumbs
1/4 cup white onion
1/4 cup mixed red and yellow bell peppers
1/4 cup lump crabmeat
1 tsp. lemon juice
1/2 tsp. Old Bay Seasoning
1/2 tsp. granulated garlic
1 large egg
salt and pepper to taste

Sauté peppers and onions and combine all ingredients. Pound chicken breasts lightly and roll with stuffing inside. Pan sear stuffed chicken until golden brown, then place in preheated 350 degree oven for 15 minutes.

. . . .

Tropical Salsa

1/2 pineapple
1 mango
1/4 honeydew melon
1/4 cantaloupe
juice of 2 limes
cifonade of 1/4 bunch fresh cilantro
3 tbsp. oilve oil
1 seeded jalapeño pepper
salt and pepper to taste

Dice all ingredients and mix together. Allow to sit for at least 4 hours refrigerated.

Roasted Leg of Lamb

bone-in leg of lamb

1 tbsp. dried jerk seasoning
1 tbsp. kosher salt
1 tbsp. black pepper
1 tbsp. dried ginger
1 tbsp. Old Bay Seasoning
1 tsp. granulated garlic
1/4 cup soy sauce

Mix together all dry ingredients. Remove all excess fat from the leg of lamb. Place in roasting pan. Pour 1/4 cup of soy sauce over the clean lamb. Rub the lamb with seasoning. Place the lamb in preheated 300 degree oven for 2-3 hours depending on desired doneness.

Sandcastle

You are at the Sandcastle on Jost van Dyke. Your sunglasses help shade the glare from the sea, the sun, and the sand that is a gleaming white you thought existed only on postcards. As you survey your surroundings from your table, barstool, beach towel, or hammock, the word exquisite pops into your mind. You don't know where to aim your camera. The atmosphere is at once peacefully removed from the "real world" as well as lively. The activity of happy holidaymakers is all around you, with reggae music in the background.

You sip your drink from the friendly bartender at The Soggy Dollar Bar, which is so named for the condition of most of the customers' money once they make their way ashore from their yachts. You watch the lunch crowd as they begin to make their way back by dinghy to the boats that dot the bay. Many will return to join the hotel guests for dinner.

Food and beverage manager Alison Logie was born in Scotland, but she is no stranger to the tropical sun after spending twenty years in South Africa. It was her daughter who convinced her to bring herself and her experience to the BVI. She loves her new post. Alison has worked with Chef Oliver Clifden, who is well known and respected on the islands. They have created a dining room that rivals the most upscale restaurants in class and style, while maintaining a casual atmosphere in which shoes are optional.

Sandcastle's Lemon Tree Chicken
(from visiting Chef, Christine Gilmour)

4 whole chicken breasts (about 12 oz. each, split, skinned and boned)
1 tsp. salt
1/8 tsp. pepper
1/4 cup all purpose flour
1/4 cup butter or margarine
1 tsp. grated lemon rind
1-2 tbsp. lemon juice
2 tbsp. dry white wine
1/2 cup heavy cream
1 cup shredded Swiss cheese (4 oz)

Rub chicken breasts thoroughly with salt and pepper. Spread flour on wax paper, turn chicken in flour to coat both sides. Heat butter in a large skillet; brown chicken breasts 4 at a time about one minute on each side; remove to a plate. Add lemon rind, lemon juice and wine to skillet; bring to a boil, stirring and scraping up browned bits. Return chicken breasts to skillet. Cover, lower heat; simmer five minutes. Arrange chicken breasts in a single layer, overlapping slightly in a 3 x 9 x 2 inch baking dish. Stir cream into wine mixture in skillet; cook until bubbly, about a minute. Pour over chicken breasts, sprinkle with Swiss cheese. Broil in pre-heated broiler, 4 inches from heat until bubbly and cheese begins to brown, about 5 minutes. This can be made ahead and broiled just before serving. Serves 6-8.

. . . .

Sautéed Shrimp in Coconut Sauce
(Resident Chef, Oliver Clifton)

2 lbs. of 16-20 shrimp, peeled and de-veined
2 tbsp. minced ginger root
5 cloves garlic, minced
2 cups coconut milk
1 cup dry white wine
salt and pepper to taste
1 tbsp. honey
1 tbsp. cilantro, minced
1 sprig thyme, minced
2 tbsp. cornstarch (diluted in 1/4 cup of cold water)
3 oz. unsalted butter

1/3 cup red bell pepper
1/3 cup green bell pepper

In a sauté pan add butter, garlic, ginger and stir about 1 minute on a medium fire. Add shrimp and stir for 1 more minute at high temperature. Add peppers, wine and coconut milk. Turn off heat and remove the shrimp to a bowl. Set aside while they are still under done. Heat sauté pan containing liquid until it simmers, thicken it with cornstarch mixture adding a little at a time to avoid over thickening. Sauce should run slowly off the back of a spoon. Add the remaining seasonings and simmer for 2-3 minutes. Finally add shrimp and turn off the heat. Re-heat briefly when you are ready to serve. Serve with boiled or steamed white rice. Optional: add a little sesame oil at the end. Serves 4-5.

. . . .

Flying Fish Sandwich

1 packet of 6-7 flying fish fillets
Seasoned salt (Season-All)
1 beaten egg
Bread crumbs

Sprinkle fish with seasoned salt. Dip into beaten egg and then bread crumbs. Fry in vegetable oil until golden brown. Serve on whole wheat bread with tartar sauce, lettuce and tomato. Add hot sauce if desired.

Baileys Irish Cream Cheesecake with Chocolate Chips

Crust:
2 cups graham cracker crumbs
6 tsp. of melted butter
1/4 cup sugar

Filling:
2 1/4 cups softened cream cheese
1 2/3 cups sugar
1 cup Baileys Irish Cream Liqueur
1 cup semi-sweet chocolate chips
5 eggs at room temperature
1 tbsp. vanilla

Icing:
1 cup cream cheese
1/2 cup powdered sugar
1/8 cup Baileys Irish Cream Liqueur

Crust:
Spray spring form pan with non-stick spray. Mix ingredients and press into pan. Bake at 325 degrees for 5-10 minutes.

Filling:
Mix all ingredients together except chocolate chips, adding eggs one at a time. Sprinkle 1/2 of the chocolate chips over crust, add filling then sprinkle remaining chocolate chips on top. Bake for 1 hour and 20 minutes. Let cool.

Icing:
Mix together and spread on cheese cake.

Makes two cakes (If you think it will be too rich with chocolate chips, just omit them.)

Cinnamon Rum French Toast

4 eggs
1 cup of milk
3 tbsp. dark rum
2 tbsp. brown sugar
1/2 tsp. cinnamon
1 pinch salt
4 tbsp. butter

Stir the ingredients together until blended. Melt butter in a large skillet. Dip 8 slices of whole wheat bread into egg mixture and then place in skillet. Fry bread over medium heat until golden brown. Sprinkle very lightly with powdered sugar for decoration, serve with maple syrup. For a nice variation serve with cream cheese AND maple syrup.

Sebastian's

ON THE BEACH

Sebastian's on the Beach was founded by an American, Cathy Sebastian, and has undergone subsequent American and European ownerships. Nevertheless, the small seaside resort has a strong, almost palpable, Caribbean feel all its own.

Rosina Augustine, manager of the resort's Seaside Grill for the last ten years, has worked in the BVI restaurant industry since she first came from St. Vincent in 1970. She knows what her customers want when they come to dine. "When you leave New York you don't want to eat New York food. The people want local food. They want the spicy West Indian food." Rosina and her Jamaican chef, Carol Wallis, oblige. Two of the more popular items on the menu (surpassed only by the garlic shrimp) are Spicy Ginger Chicken and Island Jerk Chicken. There are

some concessions to the less adventurous palate, however, such as prime rib served every Saturday night.

Vacationers seek the simple charm of a true Caribbean hotel. Folks often choose Sebastian's, on Tortola, as the ideal site for a romantic beach wedding. Rosina tells a story of a recent onsite wedding where the minister was only available in the very early morning, long before the wedding guests were to assemble that afternoon. The ceremony was simply re-enacted for the guests with Rosina standing in for the minister.

Local residents share the visitors' appreciation of the pure West Indian flavor. They come often: for the food, the fun, and sometimes just to see Rosina.

Garlic Shrimp in Paradise
(serves 1)

9 16-20 jumbo shrimp
Garlic Butter ingredients:
    6 pegs of fresh garlic
    1/2 stick celery
    1 tsp. Old Bay Seasoning
    1 pinch egg-colour
    butter

In a food processor place garlic butter ingredients and mix, it should form a paste. When finished put in a small container. Steam shrimp for 1 minute. Then add garlic butter. When it begins to melt slowly add egg-colour. Stir and serve.

. . . .

Jamaican Jerk Chicken
(serves 1)

1 8-oz. chicken
1 tsp. garlic
dash of black pepper
1 tsp. chicken base
3/4 cup red wine
4 tsp. olive oil

In a food processor puree garlic, wine, chicken base, black pepper and olive oil. Marinate chicken breast for 5 minutes then place on grill for 7 minutes on low to medium heat. Serve with jerk sauce (made of blackened seasoned blend, pimento, jerk season, tomato ketchup and B.B.Q. sauce). Garnish with fresh parsley.

Sebastian's Home Made Chocolate Cheese Cake
(serves 10)

1 1/2 cup graham crumbs
1/4 cup melted butter
1/2 lbs. cream cheese (softened)
3/4 cup sugar
1 tsp. vanilla
5 large eggs
2 egg yolks
1/4 cup heavy cream
1/2 cup small semi-sweet chocolate chips
1/4 cup Sebastian's Rum
1 cup almonds, whole or crushed as you choose

Set oven to 280 degrees and place 9-inch spring form pan in refrigerator to chill. In a large glass bowl, combine cookie crumbs, butter, 1 teaspoon of sugar and mix well. Put chocolate to melt over steam-pan. Put cream cheese and sugar in a food processor and cream fully. Add whole eggs, one at a time, whisking individually, then add vanilla, almond, Sebastian's Rum, egg yolks and heavy cream. Take spring form pan out of refrigerator, pour in mixture, then place in oven. As it bakes, slowly add melted chocolate. Bake for 15-20 minutes. Leave at room temperature to cool. Keep refrigerated.

Secret Garden

It is peace and tranquility that envelops you when you walk into the Secret Garden. The lush tropical plants, muted strains of Ella Fitzgerald in the background, comfortable seating, and welcoming soft-spoken manner of your hosts put you immediately at ease.

Owner Conrad Henley and Chef Augustine Mark met as co-workers at Peter Island and formed an immediate friendship. Their combined forty years of restaurant experience have infused the pair with both a range of skills and a shared desire to offer something different —an alternative to straight Caribbean or International cuisine.

Their product is an upscale, health-conscious, scrumptious selection of dishes that will titillate and amaze you. As an appetizer you would do well to choose the eggplant timballos or the pepper pot soup, both house specialties, followed by the sorbet served in a fresh lime shell. For the entrée you might enjoy salmon in a tamarind marinade, meat or poultry in a light sauce, one of the tasty vegetarian dishes, or even a gourmet pizza.

A fairly new restaurant, Secret Garden, in gorgeous Josiah's bay, is quickly developing a faithful clientele. Guests come for meals that are creatively and expertly prepared, with the customers' health, as well as taste buds, in mind.

Pepper Pot Soup
(serves 6)

6 cups of chicken stock
1 cup of onion, finely chopped
2 carrots, finely chopped
2 stalks celery, finely chopped
1 bay leaf
2 tbsp. salt
1 green pepper, finely chopped
2 tbsp. pepper sauce
1 cup chopped spinach
2 cloves chopped garlic
6 tbsp. flour
1/4 cup melted butter
3 tbsp. lemon juice
1 cup diced cooked chicken meat

In a large pot sauté onion, carrots, celery, green pepper, pepper sauce, garlic, and bay leaf until tender. Add chicken stock, spinach, and lemon juice. Combine butter and flour to make a roux for thickening soup. Simmer for 30 minutes then add chicken meat. Salt and pepper to taste.

Eggplant Timballos

2 large eggplants
1 tbsp. parmesan cheese
1 cup pesto
1 cup ricotta cheese
1 red pepper roasted and peeled
1 green pepper roasted and peeled
2 eggs battered
3 cups shredded mozzarella cheese

Peel eggplant then cut into layers of 1/4 in thickness, dredge in flour then dip in egg white. Sauté in oil until brown. Remove and set to cool. Combine ricotta cheese and parmesan cheese. Spread mixture on layer of eggplant, on another layer spread pesto, on another layer place a piece of red and green pepper, then place each layer on each other until you have used all of the eggplant. Top with mozzarella cheese. Place in oven and bake until cheese is brown.

Sydney's Peace & Love

NATIVE BAR & RESTAURANT

Anchor in Little Harbor on Jost van Dyke and soon Sydney will show up and invite you to dine at his dockside restaurant. He may even entice you by telling you "captains eat free". Then again maybe not, if you are only a few in your party. Going ashore he or his wife will greet you and then you have to fend for yourself. You see it is a self-service bar. You make a drink and put it in the book. Make another and add it to the list. Reservations are informal, just tell them how many and what you want for dinner, the staff will keep a look out for you and prepare your dinner when you look ready.

Dinner at Sydney's means two things, BBQ or lobster. Choices are few because you get some of everything else there is. After so many trips to the self-service bar so few choices makes sense. Diners sit on the dock overlooking the harbor and often join in each other's conversations. To describe the place as casual is an understatement. After all, what would you expect from a place whose full name is Sydney's Peace & Love Native Bar and Family Restaurant.

SYDNEY'S PEACE & LOVE

Sydney's Famous Lobster Dinner

Cut a whole lobster in half and roast until cooked with crushed garlic and butter—lots of butter. Serve the butter and garlic as a dipping sauce as well.

Serve with rice and peas
Cook kidney beans, rice, onions, parsley, and butter together until the rice is ready. Season with salt and pepper.

Also serve with Sydney's Cole Slaw
Combine cabbage, carrots, garlic and white wine together. Add pepper and mayonnaise to taste.

Don't forget the Potato Salad a la Sydney
Boiled potatos, mayo, onion, parsley, celery, red and green peppers, and salt and pepper to taste.

Top it all off with corn on the cob.

Spaghetti Junction

When John Sphultheiff and his wife, April Ridi, bought Spaghetti Junction in 1994, it was a small Italian restaurant with a big reputation. The hotspot required reservations both in season and off. For novice restaurateurs fresh from Toronto, the challenge the couple faced was not a matter of learning the tricks of running an up-and-coming restaurant in the heart of the capital, but rather how to do so at the local pace— on island time. They adapted and have built their business steadily, relocating it, nurturing it with fresh ideas, and infusing it with talented staff.

Desiree was Spaghetti Junction's cashier in the early days, but she began training with the five-star Italian chef who ran the kitchen at the time. A native of Guyana, she was a natural, and by the time the chef was ready to return to the U.S., John had no qualms about leaving his kitchen in her competent hands. "Most of the customers didn't notice," remembers John, "though a few commented on how the food just kept getting better." When asked what part of Italy his chef is from, John quips, "The Guyanese part."

Desiree has had little chance to make changes to the menu. The restaurant's customers aren't just regulars, they are hardcore devotees. In fact, they don't simply call to reserve a table; they reserve a particular meal before it runs out. Some are on a calling list where they are contacted when certain dishes are on the "Specials" list. They will tolerate no messing with the menu. A compromise is reached on Saturday nights when Pete, the young souse chef, gets to showcase his expertise.

It is clearly a strong team effort that makes Spaghetti Junction work, and John and April give their staff much credit for its success.

Cioppino

3 oz. lobster meat
2 oz. sea scallops
4 16/20 shrimp
4 sea mussels (halves)
1 tsp. olive oil
1 oz. onion, diced
1 oz. plum tomatoes, diced
1 oz. lemon juice
1/2 tsp. Italian chili flakes
1 tsp. garlic, chopped
2 oz. saffron
infused white wine
6 oz. tomato sauce
4 oz. fish stock
1 tsp. fresh basil, chopped
4 oz. fettuccine pasta, cooked
2 oz. parmesan cheese
salt and pepper to taste

Over medium to high flame, place a medium frying pan on to heat for two minutes. Pour in the olive oil, wait 30 seconds and add all of the seafood. Sauté for two minutes, add onion, tomatoes, chili flakes and garlic, sauté for a further minute. Add wine. Reduce for one minute. Add tomato sauce, lemon juice, and fish stock and bring to a boil. Add basil and simmer for one minute, adjust the seasoning and pour onto plate over pasta.

. . . .

Fruitti

3 oz. lobster meat
2 oz. sea scallops
4 16/20 shrimp
1 tsp. olive oil
1 oz. onion, diced
1 oz. plum tomato, diced
1 oz. lemon juice
1/2 tsp. Italian chili flakes
1 tsp. garlic, chopped
2 oz. white wine
8 oz. heavy cream
2 oz. fish stock

1 tsp. fresh basil, chopped
4 oz. angel hair, cooked
2 oz. parmesan cheese
salt and pepper to taste

Over medium to high flame, place a medium frying pan to heat for two minutes. Pour in the olive oil, wait 30 seconds and add all of the seafood, sauté for two minutes. Add onion, tomatoes, chili flakes and garlic... sauté for a further minute. Add white wine. Reduce for one minute. Add heavy cream, fish stock and lemon juice, bring to a boil. Add basil and parmesan cheese. Toss for one minute. Adjust the seasoning and pour onto plate over pasta.

. . . .

Jambalaya

4 oz. herbed, cooked chicken breast, sliced
4 oz. Andouille sausage, sliced
1 tsp. olive oil
1 oz. onion, diced
1 oz. mushrooms, sliced
1 oz. sundried tomatoes, (sliced)
1 oz. cajun seasoning
1/2 tsp. Italian chili flakes
1 tsp. garlic, chopped
2 oz. white wine
8 oz. heavy cream
4 oz. chicken stock
1 tsp. fresh basil, chopped
4 oz. penne rigate, cooked
2 oz. parmesan cheese

Over medium to high flame, place a medium frying pan to heat for two minutes. Pour in the olive oil, wait 30 seconds and add the chicken, sausage, mushrooms, sundried tomatoes, cajun seasoning, chili flakes and garlic. Sauté for two minutes. Add white wine. Reduce for one minute. Add heavy cream and chicken stock and bring to a boil. Add pasta, basil and parmesan cheese, toss for one minute, adjust the seasoning and pour onto plate.

99

The Sugar Mill

Tucked in on a hillside in Little Apple Bay may be one of the best restaurants you will ever find. The Sugar Mill is a small hotel with a huge reputation. Owned by Jinx and Jeff Morgan, the restaurant is set in a 370-year-old sugar mill. Surrounding this stunning building, the Gazebo Bar and the Terrace Breakfast dinning room is a lush tropical garden. The views are of the beach and Jost van Dyke and the sunsets are not to be missed. It is, however, the food that brings people back time and again. It is a fusion of West Indian and European/American done in a most unique way. Many places in the BVI use local ingredients but few do it so creatively. How about a plate of black bean pancakes with vegetable salsa.

The Morgans are regular Gourmet Magazine contributors and their restaurant has been voted one of the best in the Caribbean in several magazine polls and by food critics throughout the world. If you go be prepared to spend a long delightful evening. It is not that the service is slow, au contraire; you just won't want to leave.

Grilled Quail with Mango-Papaya Sauce
(serves 6)

Boned quail is becoming more available all over the country. If you can't find them, this preparation is equally good made with Cornish game hens.

12 boned quail or 6 Cornish game hens

Marinade:
1 cup oil
1/4 cup sherry or cider vinegar
1/4 cup orange juice
1 clove garlic
1 tbsp. fresh or 1 tsp. dried tarragon
1 tbsp. fresh or 1 tsp. dried basil
salt and pepper

Sauce:
1 large mango, peeled, seeded and minced
1 large papaya, peeled, seeded and minced
1 tsp. red pepper flakes
1/2 jalapeño pepper, seeded and minced
juice of 2 limes
salt and pepper

Whisk together all marinade ingredients in a bowl and marinate quail for 2 to 3 hours at room temperature or overnight in the refrigerator. Grill the quail for 3 to 4 minutes on each side for rare or 5 to 6 minutes for medium.

To make sauce, stir together all ingredients and serve cold with the hot quail.

Plantains with Caviar
(serves 6)

1/2 cup dried black beans
1 small onion
1 clove garlic, peeled
1 tsp. salt
3 ripe plantains
2 cups vegetable or peanut oil
1 cup sour cream
6 oz. red caviar
6 oz. black caviar
1 red onion, peeled and sliced into thin rings

Wash the beans well in a strainer and pick over to remove any grit. Place in a covered saucepan with the onion, garlic, salt and 3 cups cold water. Bring beans to a boil and simmer, covered, for about 2 1/2 hours, or until they are tender but not mushy. Remove onion and garlic and drain well. Mash beans with a fork.

Peel plantains and cut on the diagonal into 1/2-inch thick slices. Soak in salted water for 30 minutes. Pat dry with paper towels. Heat oil in a deep skillet and when hot add the slices of plantain. Fry until golden then drain on paper towels. Press with the back of a spoon until they are 1/4-inch thick. Refry for 30 seconds and drain well on paper towels.

Place a row of plantain slices down the center of a plate or platter with stripes of the beans, some cream and two caviars beside them. Garnish with red onion rings.

. . . .

Piña Colada Cake

Even those who don't know much about the Caribbean have heard of that smooth, grown up milkshake, the Piña Colada. Here the same flavors appear in a cake that is sure to bring diners back for seconds.

6 egg whites
1 1/2 cups sugar
4 egg yolks
1/2 cup vegetable oil
1/2 cup water

1 tsp. vanilla
1 1/2 cups flour
3 tsp. baking powder
dash salt
1/4 cup pineapple juice
2 tbsp. white rum
1/4 cup cream of coconut

Frosting:
6 tbsp. butter
1 lb. confectioners sugar, sifted
1 egg
1/4 cup cream
1 tsp. vanilla
1 tsp. coconut or almond extract
8 oz. shredded coconut

Preheat oven to 350 degrees. Beat egg whites until soft peaks form. Gradually add 1/2 cup sugar while continuing to beat until very stiff. Whisk together egg yolks, oil, water and vanilla in a small bowl. Sift together sugar, flour, baking powder and salt. Fold flour mixture into beaten yolks and mix well. Fold in beaten egg whites. Pour into two 8-inch cake pans. Bake for about 25 minutes at 350 degrees until sides shrink and top springs back when touched. Turn out and cool on cake racks. In a small bowl, mix together pineapple juice, rum and cream of coconut. Brush both cake layers with this combination. Beat together butter, confectioners sugar, egg, cream, vanilla and coconut extract until smooth and creamy. Combine half of this frosting with 1/4 cup crushed pineapple and spread between layers as a filling. Stir 1 tablespoon dark rum into remaining frosting. Frost cake and sprinkle top with toasted coconut.

Tamarind Club

One of the things that makes the BVI such a magical place to visit, especially for boaters, is the countless number of bays that line the miles of coasts. To single out any one bay as particularly beautiful would be very difficult indeed. Yet most visitors to Josiah's Bay in Tortola have no problem proclaiming its beauty to be outstanding. Perched above the gorgeous bay is the Tamarind Club.

The Tamarind Club is a small hotel with a popular restaurant that is open to the public. Besides the spectacular view, diners come to enjoy a menu that varies almost daily, a result of Dawn's focus on utilizing available fresh fruit, vegetables, and fish. Guests also come for the more consistent house specials such as crab cakes, rack of lamb, and swordfish.

Watching the guests sitting back in their wicker chairs after Sunday Brunch (reservations a must), or bobbing in the pool while sipping frozen daiquiris by the swim-up bar, you will notice that they all seem to wear the same satisfied, "this is how I imagined the Caribbean" smile.

Tamarind Club Paella
(serves 4)

Paella is a great Spanish dish which we serve a lot of at the Tamarind Club. In addition many Caribbean cultures have Paella or Pilau as it is known, in one form or another in their local cuisine.

 1 large yellow onion, medium diced
 5 cups parboiled rice
 1/2 tbsp. saffron threads
 1/2 lb. peeled and deviened 16/20 shrimps
 1/4 lb. 10/20 count scallops
 1/4 lb. cleaned and tubed squid, cut into rings
 3 8-oz. chicken breasts cut into bite size pieces
 1 8-oz. tin crushed tomatoes
 1/4 spicy sausage cut into 1/2 inch pieces
 1/4 lb. unsalted butter
 1/8 cup extra virgin olive oil
 salt and pepper to taste
 water or chicken stock
 10 cloves chopped garlic (or as much or as little as you like)

In a large heavy bottomed frying pan sauté diced onions in butter, olive oil and salt & pepper. Add rice, saffron and enough liquid to cover rice by 2 inches and cook rice over medium to high heat until rice is 3/4 done, then allow rice to stand and cool. In separate pans sauté all food items with butter, olive oil, chopped garlic and salt pepper until 3/4 done except for chicken and sausage which must be cooked all the way through. When the rice has cooled place in a large heavy bottomed pan. Add stock and chopped tomatoes, 1/2 cup at a time. Add all seafood, chicken and sausage and cook until seafood is cooked all the way through and the rice has absorbed all the flavors of the pan. The rice should be moist but not wet and have somewhat of a reddish colour.

Tamarind Baked Salmon

 1 6-oz. piece of fresh salmon
 2 tbsp. local tamarind syrup
 1 tsp. salt
 1 tbsp. pepper

Season salmon with salt and pepper. Place salmon on a greased pan and bake in oven at 350 degrees for 3 minutes, then pour tamarind syrup over salmon and return to oven for 2 more minutes. Remove and serve on cushion of bean salsa.

Salsa:
 1 cup black beans
 1 cup red beans
 1 cup chopped green pepper
 1 cup chopped red pepper
 2 tbsp. sugar
 1 tbsp. vinegar
 2 tbsp. fresh cilantro
 1 tbsp. hot pepper sauce
 1 tbsp. olive oil

In a bowl combine all the ingredients and mix well. Can be served warm or cold.

Thelma's Hideout

The sign on the wall of Thelma's Hideout reads "Established ...." (too long ago to remember), which makes it the oldest bar and restaurant in Virgin Gorda. It is a slightly rambling series of enclosures and open courtyard areas with simple furnishings and lush greenery. It is the epitome of rustic charm.

But it is Thelma King who makes the Hideout the unique establishment that it is. She is here all day, every day, cooking in the kitchen, serving behind the bar, or passing a quiet afternoon with regular customers on the shaded front porch. It is hard to imagine Thelma's Hideout without Miss Thelma.

Though born into the family establishment in the thirties, it was only twenty years ago that Thelma made the Hideout her own. Most of her life has been spent very far from home. From her childhood at school in Antigua, to her adult years traveling as a personal chef to the Major family, Thelma has indulged in a passion to go, see, and do. By the time her family needed her to return to the family business, Thelma was ready for the challenge.

The most widely appreciated result of her "getaway years" is her fine cooking abilities. The food at Thelma's, like Thelma herself, is a delectable mix of Caribbean know-how and worldly finesse. The simplest of dishes, such as baked chicken or BBQ ribs, taste home-cooked and exceptional at the same time. The menu is limited to three dishes per day and dinner must be ordered by 3:00 pm, but diners seldom feel limited. Miss Thelma's flexibility ensures her customers' pleasure and satisfaction.

Though you don't see Thelma's Hideout advertised, it is by no means unknown. Residents come from throughout the BVI, and guests from the local resorts and hotels are sent here for a special treat. Even the New York Times knows about Thelma's Hideout and has recommended it. Well, no one ever said it was a secret hideout.

Top of the Baths

At sixteen, Charlene Henderson knew what wanted: her own restaurant, and where she wanted it: at the Baths. This is not an impossible dream, especially when the Baths happens to be on family land. While the Henderson's had given the land to the BVI for Virgin Gorda's most popular National Park, the fact that part of the property would be Charlene's restaurant was understood. The exact location became an issue that took nearly twenty-five years to resolve.

Charlene used this time to gain and sharpen her business skills. By the time she got the go ahead, she was more than ready for the responsibilities of a restaurant. She and her husband, Norman, built their complex in record time and opened the Top of the Baths in 1994.

Charlene has gathered an exceptionally talented staff. They are a competent, creative and likeable group. Most have been there from the beginning and so they form a strong, cohesive team. Everyone brings ideas for the unique menu and "Tall Boy", the head chef, pulls it all together with finesse. Charlene calls it, "international with a Caribbean twist," which is an apt description as there are dishes such as green banana salad, conch burgers, and egg roles stuffed with avocado or spicy chicken and black beans. "We want our guests to experience the Caribbean through our food," Charlene explains. That must be exactly what the guests want, because they keep coming back.

Green Banana Salad

5 lbs. green bananas
1 green pepper
1 red pepper
1 small red onion
1 tbsp. black olives
4 tbsp. olive oil
salt and pepper

Boil bananas (checking consistency to avoid stiffness) in water, salt, and vinegar (to keep browning). Cool, peel and slice into thin medallions. Chop vegetables. Toss with banana slices and oil, add salt and pepper to taste. Serve immediately.

. . . .

Conch Burgers

5 lbs. raw conch
1 cup onion
1 cup green pepper
1/2 cup red pepper
1 cup celery
1/4 cup dried thyme
5 tbsp. chopped garlic
2 tsp. black pepper
1/2 tbsp. lemon pepper
2 1/2 cup rolled oats
6 1/2 cups bread crumbs
1/2 tbsp. lime juice
3 1/2 tbsp. Lowry's Seasoning Salt
5 eggs

Skin conch and grind in food processor. Chop vegetables in food processor. Mix all ingredients together (hold back 1/2 cup oats). Roll and cut into 4 oz. pieces. Shape into patties, using extra oats to hold shape. Cook on hot grill for no more than 5 minutes.

William Thornton

(WILLIE T)

The William Thornton, known fondly as the Willie T, is a floating bar and restaurant anchored in the Bight at Norman Island. Built in 1985, it is a replica of an old Great Lakes Schooner. Owned and operated by New Zealander Nick Gardiner and Scotsman Ewan Anderson, the Willie T has earned, over the past 18 years, a reputation for its wild parties. There you'll find loud music, body shots, and revellers leaping off decks into the sea. This may not be everyone's cup of tea, but it is obviously a lot of people's, as its popularity just keeps growing.

That's the bar, but what about the restaurant? You won't find hotdogs and pizza there. Instead, there's plenty of Oriental Calamari, Ceviche, Jumbo Garlic Prawns, and Rum Chili Baby Back Ribs. And don't forget the big favourite, coconut rum-flavoured chicken roti.

The chefs at the Willie T don't strive to compete with the attraction of the bar. Rather, they use it as an opportunity to surprise and impress large numbers of unsuspecting diners. Chefs Kevin and Delphi, who are from very different backgrounds (Canadian and West Indian, respectively), combine their skills and experience to produce a menu that can stand among Willie T's more sedate competitors.

And who out there can match the setting of the dining room? The Willie T, swaying gently on a single anchor, is the only restaurant in the BVI with a three hundred and sixty degree view.

Chicken Roti

Par boil some cubed potatoes. Sauté 3 or 4 boneless chicken breasts with 1/4 cup curry powder and some onions. When almost cooked add 2-3 oz of coconut rum. Add the potatoes and simmer slowly until tender and let cool.

Wraps:
Boil some yellow peas, drain and crush in a mill. Add fresh garlic, onion, cumin, salt and a bit of baking powder. Knead into some flour, adding water until it is stiff but can be rolled out. Roll thin in a circle and fry in olive oil at a high temp. Turn once and set aside to cool Put the chicken/potato mixture in the wrap, heat and serve with mango chutney.

Rice Pilaf

Cook 2 cups of white rice in 4 cups of chicken stock. Add 1/4 cup of V-8 juice. Add chopped celery, red and green peppers, onions, parsley, salt and pepper.

....

Bourbon Peppercorn Sauce for Meats

Make a demi glase from veal bones, or beef bones simmered all day with celery, carrots, onion, salt and pepper. Reduce to 1/4 or less. Add crushed black peppercorns to taste or about 1 oz. Pour the bourbon until you think it is enough and then remember this is a Willy T special and pour some more.

Index

CONVERSION TABLE

U.S. to Metric

Capacity:

1/5 tsp.	= 1 ml
1 tsp.	= 5 ml
1 tbsp.	= 15 ml
1 fluid oz.	= 30 ml
1/5 cup	= 50 ml
1 cup	= 240 ml
2 cups (1 pint)	= 470 ml
4 cups (1 quart)	= .95 liter
4 quarts (1 gal.)	= 3.8 liters
1 tbsp.	= 1.5 cl

Weight:

1 oz.	= 28 grams
1 lb.	= 454 grams

. . . .

Metric to U.S.

Capacity:

1 ml	= 1/5 tsp.
5 ml	= 1 tsp.
15 ml	= 1 tbsp.
30 ml	= 1 fluid oz.
100 ml	= 3.4 fluid oz.
240 ml	= 1 cup
1 liter	= 34 fluid oz.
1 liter	= 4.2 cups
1 liter	= 2.1 pints
1 liter	= 1.06 quarts
1 liter	= .26 gallon

Weight:

1 gram	= .035 oz.
100 grams	= 3.5 oz.
500 grams	= 1.10 lbs.
1 kilogram	= 2.205 lbs.
1 kilogram	= 35 oz.

Cooking Measurement Equivalents

16 tbsp.	= 1 cup
12 tbsp.	= 3/4 cup
10 tbsp. + 2 tsp.	= 3/4 cup
8 tbsp.	= 1/2 cup
6 tbsp.	= 3/8 cup
5 tbsp. + 1 tsp.	= 1/3 cup
4 tbsp.	= 1/4 cup
2 tbsp.	= 1/8 cup
2 tbsp. + 2 tsp.	= 1/6 cup
1 tbsp.	= 1/16 cup
2 cups	= 1 pint
2 pints	= 1 quart
3 tsp.	= 1 tbsp.
48 tsp.	= 1 cup